What People Are S

Agile for Non-Software Teams

Finally, we have an Agile book for non-software teams! In this book, Gil Broza has taken Agile values, principles, and practices and translated them to be useful to teams of any type – from marketing teams to management teams and beyond. As technology disrupts industry after industry, teams of all kinds are facing increasing complexity and uncertainty, and must learn how to succeed in this environment. Gil's book is a great place to start that journey.

~ **Jim Highsmith**, Executive Consultant, ThoughtWorks, coauthor of *EDGE* and *The Agile Manifesto*

This book is a practical, well-written, and immediately applicable guide to becoming more Agile in a non-software context. Complete with helpful examples, just enough theory, and down-to-earth prose, reading it is like having the author sit down with you over coffee and help you chart a pragmatic path to agility that's right for your unique business context.

~ **Jorgen Hesselberg**, author of *Unlocking Agility*

This book is an easy read, with short and concise chapters full of practical and tangible recommendations. I can safely recommend it to non-software teams eager to get started exploring the opportunities of Agile.

~ **Malene Krohn**, SVP, SimCorp

I wish I had this book back when I started my Agile journey.

~ **Breanna Ramos**, HR Associate, TechSmith

I discovered that my branding and graphic design team naturally works with some Agile principles, but with a more thoughtful and considered approach to our mind-set and processes, we could go from being sort-of-Agile to truly Agile.

~ **Chris Armstrong**, Design Director, Operative Brand Consulting

Gil has moved the needle on solving the problem of "how can non-software teams adopt an Agile way of working" by providing an easy-to-follow, step-by-step pathway forward.

~ **Jeremy Pasley**, PMO Manager, Global Program Management, Caterpillar

I'm in the process of leading an Agile transformation at a pharmaceutical company – the first of its kind in such an industry. I read this book in one evening and found myself nodding in agreement the whole way through. Gil has clearly pinpointed every key thing you will see, hear, and feel throughout such a transformation in a non-software environment, and how to work your way through it. I wish such a resource had been available at the start of our transformation!

~ **Heather Francis**, Head of Transformation, Roche Canada

There are so many opportunities to apply Agile approaches beyond the realm of software development. But how? Thanks to Gil, there's now a practical pathway to making it work. This is a resource I will regularly recommend!

~ **Andy Kaufman**, Host of the *People and Projects Podcast*

I have known Gil to be a thoughtful practitioner of Agile principles. In this book, Gil provides what so many leaders have asked me for: a non-software approach for employing Agile for better outcomes. He does so with practicality and without sacrificing depth.

~ **Lyssa Adkins**, Agile & Leadership Coach, LyssaAdkins.com, author of *Coaching Agile Teams*

Gil gives a new perspective on the transformation process by showing the importance of the mind-set necessary for Agile to be successful. Whether you are a manager or team member, this guide will give you a roadmap on how an Agile transformation might work for you.

~ **Omar A. Acuna Jr.**, CSM, PTC Therapeutics

This book fits with my experiences coaching non-technical Agile teams. Its conversational style, examples, and explanations will resonate with any non-software reader.

~ **Anthony Register**, Business Agility Coach

Agile thinking and practice brings benefits to all kinds of work outside of tech, but sometimes the software-centred jargon gets in the way. This book offers clear and practical advice to help your team figure out your Agile way of working in order to reap the benefits of increased focus, faster feedback, and happier people.

~ **Ellen Grove**, Business Agility Coach

Working in a non-IT environment and interested in starting with Agile? Don't know exactly how, or whether it would fit for you? I have supported several teams like yours. This book is your starting point and guidance for the journey, helping you figure out the best way of working for your context.

~ **Kerstin Bresler**, Agile Coach

As more and more organizations transform nontechnical teams to Agile, it's now apparent that this is a different animal than transforming software development teams. This practical resource is a must-have for this kind of endeavor.
~ **John Hill**, Agile Coach and Trainer

Business agility is the superpower of success in a rapidly changing world. Gil's latest title will inspire you to begin, accelerate, or adapt your Agile journey to achieve the next summit of your own climb to the top! I use Gil's prior works in my role for a Fortune 100 company, and as required reading for my university graduate and undergraduate courses.
~ **Kevin D. Martin**, Director, Enterprise Security Group, USAA, and Lecturer, University of Texas - San Antonio

This book is written for the audience we always forget in Agile transformations: the non-software roles. It's the first book I've seen that really tackles that elephant in the room. Read it to learn where to start to put agility in those functions, because it's only when all of these come together that you get true organizational agility.
~ **David Dame**, VP, Global Agile, Scotiabank

Despite emerging in the technology domain, there is nothing exclusively tech about Agile. If there is any uncertainty in your work outcomes – and let's face it, that's all work these days – then an Agile approach will both improve customer outcomes and de-risk the work. With this book, Gil has created a practical and insightful guide for any team, in any part of the organization, seeking to be Agile.
~ **Evan Leybourn**, Founder & CEO, Business Agility Institute

There's a strong focus on principles rather than particular frameworks, and Gil provides many practical tips for why, when, and how to introduce and sustain Agile. In this time of Agile being considered everywhere, Gil has managed to make Agile accessible to everyone.
~ **Sandy Mamoli**, coauthor of *Creating Great Teams* and Agile Advisor at Nomad8

You'll instantly feel as if you're having a conversation with an experienced partner who deeply understands Agile and business. Gil has a knack for providing just the right background information, helping you connect the dots with many practical real-life business examples while offering you a host of options from which to start or deepen your journey. You will be in the driver's seat throughout, choosing what fits for your situation and unique goals.
~ **Suzanne Daigle**, Business Strategist and Partner, NuFocus Strategic Group

AGILE for
NON-SOFTWARE
TEAMS

A Practical Guide for Your Journey

GIL BROZA

Foreword by **L. David Marquet**, author of *Turn the Ship Around!*

Agile for Non-Software Teams
A Practical Guide for Your Journey

The publisher offers discounts on this book when ordered in quantity for bulk purchases or special sales, which may include electronic versions and/or custom covers and content particular to your business, training goals, marketing focus, and branding interests. For more information, please contact:

> Gil Broza
> (416) 302-8120
> gil@3PVantage.com

Published by 3P Vantage Media
Copyright © 2019 Gil Broza. All rights reserved.

ISBN: 978-0-9880016-5-7

Cover Art: Galia Broza
Cover and Interior Design: Christopher & Heather Kirk, GFSstudio.com
Editing: Mark Woodworth
Proofreading: Jennifer Flaxman

CONTENTS

FOREWORD

by L. David Marquet

When I took command of the nuclear submarine USS *Santa Fe*, I had a problem. I was trained for a different type of submarine, and my crew was trained to follow orders.

That didn't work.

Instead of leaning *in*, I had to learn how to lean *back*, creating the space for my team to lean toward me and bring forward their ideas. This created a powerful sense of ownership and responsibility. Some people called it empowerment.

We did this by changing the way we worked. More specifically, we did it by changing the language we used. We changed the language in three different ways:

1. We replaced the language of command and control with that of initiative, proactivity, responsibility, and ownership. The key here was "intent": the team would come to me and state their intentions rather than having me give them instructions. "Intent" became a magic word for us. If you spoke that word, as in, "I intend to submerge the submarine," that meant you already had permission. As commander, I could ask questions, I could veto an action, but in the absence of vetoing, it meant you had permission to move forward.

2. We changed the team's common language from that of proving and doing to one of improving and learning. Whereas in

the past we had been so proud of being a "can-do" organization, we needed to add some "can-think." We wrapped the thinking around the doing. I visualized work as a sequence of *decide-do-reflect*.

3. We replaced a language of invulnerability and certainty with one of vulnerability and uncertainty. We practiced saying things like "This could be wrong if..." or "This plan is based on the following assumptions..." and finally, "I don't know."

We stopped calling our training program a "training program" and started calling it a "learning program." Not only did this create the right emphasis but it shifted the onus from the trainer, whose obligation was to impart training upon people, to the learners, who were invited to enhance their own skills.

The results were remarkable, with the submarine setting records for crew retention and morale, on the one hand, and performance on the other.

Even more remarkable was what happened over the next decade: no fewer than 10 of the officers were selected to command their own submarines. That shows that this way of treating people was better not only for the organization in the short run, but also for the people in the organization in the long run.

When I told the story, some people said this was "Agile." Agile is not a word you commonly associated with nuclear submarines. But the idea of thinking about the work in chunks, an emphasis on learning, and letting the team make decisions are all parts of the underpinnings of Agile. In short, the people who would normally be assigned to the "doing" become the "deciders."

The world is changing, and work life is changing. People are more educated and work is becoming more cognitive, creative, and thoughtful. The drudgery of performing repetitive mindless tasks, which was once a hallmark of the industrial age, is fading away. As that happens, workplaces that can tap into the creativity and the thinking of their people will win.

This is why Agile works — but Agile is *not* about software. Agile is an approach for releasing our human instinct to solve problems for a meaningful purpose. It is about putting the doers in charge. Sure, it's a better way of doing software. It's also a better way of running your business. And I believe it's a better way of running your life.

This book is timely.

Agile, which started and grew in the software development business, is now spreading to other parts of the organization that are not involved directly with software. Additionally, Agile transformations are reaching higher into the organization, bumping up against people who are unfamiliar with the terms. This book will help there.

I love this book for a number of reasons:

It's accessible. As Gil Broza illuminates the concepts of Agile — the philosophy, the culture, and the way of working — he steers clear of jargon and doesn't get hung up. Although he focuses this book on Agile in the workplace, he talks about it in a way that can be applied in any domain, including our personal lives.

It's unpretentious. It imparts its wisdom in a semiplayful way that opens the door to experimentation and a learning mind-set. We don't get deterred by the heaviness of initiatives we have to win at.

It provides specific tools. Too many books leave the reader to figure out what to actually *do*. Here, while respecting the reader's intelligence, Gil provides a pathway, along with actionable advice that you and your team can try.

I hope you enjoy this book as much as I have done. Even more important, I hope you apply some of its tools and concepts to make your workplace better for the humans who inhabit it.

L. David Marquet
@ldavidmarquet

INTRODUCTION

In 2000, I became a development team manager for the first time. I didn't know how to manage either work or people, so I took courses, read books, learned to use Microsoft Project, and observed other managers around me. In short order, I realized I didn't want to adhere to most of the concepts I learned. In particular, centralized, top-down, know-it-all planning troubled me. I had just spent years on the receiving end of it, and it didn't feel right.

I decided to use other methods. Instead of the mind-numbing weekly status meeting, my team had a quick daily meeting where we identified the next most-important tasks and folks coordinated with each other. I visited each team member every day, learning about them, listening to their problems, and collaboratively coming up with solutions. I forged ties with my counterparts in technical support and product management to understand what our customers were really asking for (which, one day, earned me an earful from the VP about "going around her"). I didn't have a name for my approach, but it felt right. One year later, interviewing for the bioinformatics team management position at a scientific production company, I told my future boss I would take the role only if I could use this approach, which I now knew to be called eXtreme Programming. He said yes, and he was true to his word.

My new team liked the methods. We evolved them, first based on instinct, then on the guidance of an article we found on the Internet, and ultimately based on books and conferences. We rescued the outsourced project we had inherited, and we went on to deliver value incrementally. We knew now that our approach was called "Agile" and that it was a real thing. In 2004, wanting to help more companies and professionals enjoy the benefits of Agile with less thrashing, I became an Agile coach, trainer, and consultant.

Fast-forward a decade plus, and the landscape today couldn't be more different. Almost everyone in business has heard about Agile, or at least about a specific form of it called Scrum. Everywhere you look, there are frameworks, conferences, meetups, books, consultants, courses, certifications, and blogs. Agile has survived longer than many management ideas and shows no signs of going away. Everybody's doing it, right?

Well, not quite. It's still mostly people in software development and IT who use Agile. However, more and more executives have been seeing its benefits, and "agile transformation" and "business agility" are on everyone's lips. Many nontech managers now have a mandate, or an expectation, to become agile. Even if we ignore for a moment that mandated agility has a very low success rate, something extremely important is missing.

From my vantage point, nontech leaders are finding themselves in the same position I was in 2000–2004. Adopting an Agile way of working is a viable proposition, and leadership is usually supportive, but... a plethora of questions arise. What's a good way to start a team on Agile? Which aspects deserve attention, and of what kind? How can it go wrong, and what are appropriate responses? As contrasted with the beginning of the century, a multitude of learning resources is available now, though they almost exclusively address software development situations. Another difference is the existence of many frameworks that promise context-free shortcuts to agility without the discomfort of growing it organically. Attractive and popular as they are, neither are they suitable for every pursuit nor do they tell the full story.

I have worked with non-software teams for quite some time as trainer, coach, and consultant. I see the immense diversity of business and human landscapes, realize that no single way of working can cover all of them, and appreciate that Agile may not be a good fit for some. I've written this book to give you and your team a **pathway for considering, designing, starting, growing, and sustaining an Agile way of working** — all without prescribing a single choice for your particular situation. I believe that you're well capable of designing effective methods without being a process expert, and that you should own the choices — because you'll have to live with the results! Rather than impose a drag-and-drop solution, however, I offer a tested thought-process, some hard-earned wisdom, and a great number of reality checks.

Since we're talking about bringing in change, I assume that you're managing or leading one or more teams in your area. Don't use your position to impose Agile on them, as that's a nonstarter; instead, think of yourself as a host, inviting people to a shared experience. The book is organized chronologically, with each chapter corresponding to a key step in the months-long (sometimes even years-long) collaborative pathway of creating that experience. I suggest that you read one chapter at a time and act on its guidance (which usually involves conversations, workshops, and reflection); the chapter's closing text will indicate what needs to be in place for you to continue with the next chapter. If you're an executive, however, an early read through chapters 1, 2, 5, 6, and 7 will give you a clear picture of what your manager(s) and their teams will be going through — and what support they might need along the way. Alternatively, if you're part of a management team that's curious about Agile, you'd benefit from the book club approach, reading the book chapter by chapter and discussing each one as you go along.

Here is the pathway: you'll start by learning why choosing a way of working is important (chapter 1) and by considering what's special about the Agile option (chapter 2). You'll discuss the possibility of using Agile with your team; they will inevitably have concerns, which I'll help you think through (chapter 3). You'll determine where to experiment with Agile for the first time (chapter 4), but before you change anything about your methods, you'll need to understand why "becoming Agile" is a journey, how it can go wrong, and how to prepare yourself and others for it (chapters 5 and 6). You'll learn just enough about certain Agile principles (chapter 7) to design your initial way of working (chapter 8) and get going. You'll see what it takes to strategically support your team in the first few months (chapter 9). Once you get the hang of Agile and want more of it, I'll have plenty of advice, ideas, and warnings for you (chapter 10). If you're curious, the epilogue will give you a glimpse into a possible future of agility across the organization. You'll find additional inspiration and examples in an appendix containing several success-and-struggle stories from the field, describing how entire non-software groups went Agile.

This book could have been long, detailed, and theoretical. I have chosen instead to make it concise, direct, and practical, so that you're more likely to pick it up, read it, and take it on your Agile journey. I have made it as pure-protein as possible, with just enough theory to guide your choices and empower you to act. As a result, some deep insights and powerful messages, to which other Agile books dedicate entire chapters, appear as single sentences. The book won't tell you *everything* about Agile or discuss every wrinkle, because I want you to minimize studying while maximizing preparation. Where applicable, it includes references to additional books, including — of course :-) — my own books: *The Agile Mind-Set* and *The Human Side of Agile*.

Ready to start? Let's dive in.

Gil Broza, Toronto, 2019

gil@3PVantage.com

3PVantage.com

Chapter 1
How Your Way of Working Matters

You Can Reach Your Goals in Multiple Ways

Consider the following three unrelated scenarios. What would you do in each?

1. You're in charge of marketing an innovative new product. Your team has tested their campaign ideas with a focus group, and now you're compiling a report for stakeholders and executives. Will you provide detailed analyses and nice charts, or a summary with some highlights, or perhaps a yes-no-maybe conclusion with the promise of further insights upon request?

2. Your house needs renovations. You're planning to completely modernize the kitchen and the main bathroom, remodel all the bedrooms, and upgrade several windows. You've found an interior designer and a general contractor whom you like. Will you obtain a detailed design, get the contractor to price it and commit to dates, and rent a place while the crew is working? Or will you obtain a rough design and pricing for each major change, prioritize the changes, and have the contractor perform them one at a time while you still live in the house?

3. You want to throw a big party for a loved one's major birthday, with dozens of guests, a three-course meal, live music, and a "this-is-your-life!" video. The birthday is one month away. Will you: Do what it takes to ensure that all these elements fall into place? Choose just a couple of elements and make them really special? Start with a budget and see what you can fit in? Make backup plans in case a lot of people can't attend due to the short notice?

In all three scenarios, you're spending time doing work that matters. Your stakeholders will have an assessment of the potential campaign, your house will better fit your current taste and needs, and you'll create a memorable experience for your loved one.

The questions posed for each scenario demonstrate that there are multiple ways to produce those results. *Each of those ways of working optimizes for something different.* If you compile a detailed feedback report, you optimize for its readers' ability to make an informed decision. Renovating a home one upgrade at a time will allow you to stop if the costs balloon, and to change your mind as the work progresses. By making a big detailed plan for the birthday party, you mitigate various risks.

Whatever you optimize for, the choice will have disadvantages. A full report might take a while to prepare and be wasted work if the conclusion is a clear "yes" or "no." Incremental renovations might not get you everything you want. A detailed birthday plan might require extensive changes once you contact event venues, caterers, and bands.

All ways of working have pros and cons. To complicate things further, there isn't always an obvious best choice. Even if you need to do similar work again, the context for it might justify a different way of working. However, we human beings are creatures of habit, and sometimes we default to familiar, popular, or presumably obvious ways of working. But then, if our results fall short of expectations, we're not likely to question our own methods. This is quite evident in organizations (all staffed by actual humans!) that strive to follow accepted wisdom and "best practices."

Without changing the basic work activities, you can be more effective, efficient, and successful by being *intentional* about your way of working: how you plan, decide what to do next, engage individuals and teams, perform tasks, adapt to changes, and so on. This concept applies anytime you spend effort doing something that delivers a desired result, whether personally or professionally, paid or unpaid, voluntarily or under mandate, either with others or on your own.

This book focuses on professional, paid work that involves others. It will help you see where and how an *Agile* way of working can help your business accomplish better outcomes. And it will help you get there with minimal risk and thrashing about.

The Potential of an Agile Way of Working

Your line of work probably has established ways of working. For example, every office building is different from the next, but the *process for constructing* them has been in place for decades. In another example, every person has unique health challenges, but the *process for diagnosing* them is rather standard.

Nevertheless, ways of working may change over time. Some undergo gradual improvement, while others are transformed. To continue the previous examples, both construction and medicine don't operate exactly the way they did 100 years ago. Scientific and technological progress explains only part of the change. Other partial explanations are the evolution of business models, enormous economic growth, and vast changes in societal norms and people's expectations.

This kind of evolution has been happening in software development over the last 20 years. That field emerged as a veritable profession and business domain only in the 1970s, and by the 1980s software development was already being managed in standard ways that resembled traditional project management. Despite being accepted wisdom, the usual method, called "Waterfall," was not consistently successful. Most projects ended late, over-budget, or off the mark. And on a personal level, most of the people involved, such as analysts, programmers, testers, and managers, were not enjoying the process. By the mid-1990s, some of them were trying to do things differently: empowering cross-functional teams, lightening the process load, forging closer ties with their customers, and delivering results and adapting to change more frequently. In 2001, 17 of those thought leaders captured the gist of their ideas in the Manifesto for Agile Software Development.[1]

Conferences and books on Agile development appeared. Companies developed new tools for managing and executing Agile projects. More and more, organizations reported that Agile helped them improve business outcomes. In the case of companies building technologies for other businesses or for the mass market, that often meant retaining and gaining market share, fulfilling customers' needs earlier, and adapting quickly to shifting landscapes. Organizations developing internal-use solutions saw greater IT-Business collaboration and solutions that better suited their purpose. Both kinds of organizations often experienced increased employee engagement, higher transparency within and across functions, easier prioritization and planning, greater application of team members' skills and smarts, and altogether wiser use of their time. Many workers and managers, who did not enjoy the Waterfall method and the command-and-control structure that often accompanied it, found their passion again.

This result has, alas, not been ubiquitous. Many companies continue to struggle to work in an Agile way, and many that believed they'd implemented it correctly haven't seen much improvement. The reasons vary, but three seem universal: they adopted Agile practices while continuing to make the same strategic and managerial choices as before; they "installed" rigid processes without adapting them to context; and they received insufficient support from leadership.

An important misperception has also contributed to the struggles and disenchantment. Agile has a fundamental worldview: healthy teams that consistently delight customers will achieve great business results. Unfortunately, many organizations have gravitated to Agile believing it's an installable methodology for expediting techies' work. Their executives came to expect "cheaper, better, faster," and their teams were supposed to "sprint" and to "increase velocity." They didn't realize that saving costs and compressing schedules are secondary — and not guaranteed — effects of something deeper: that customer-oriented Agile teams stop (or sometimes never start) working on useless deliverables. Because this reason is not immediately evident in popular Agile processes, teams assumed they'd achieve speed by skimping on activities that (incorrectly) seem to matter less, such as design, testing, and documentation. The resulting long-term pains eclipsed their short-term gains.

Despite the mixed results, businesses that are serious about *being* Agile in software development generally see improved outcomes. In fact, many professionals attribute their feelings of pride, accomplishment, connection, and even joy to being Agile, and they never want to go back to traditional methods. Which raises the question: Why limit its application to software? After all, some practices clearly carry over to other kinds of work. More significantly, the principles behind those practices, as well as the values behind the principles, have wider applicability. Indeed, Agile is now being used in ever more non-software functions and initiatives, where it's increasingly demonstrating its effectiveness in improving business outcomes.

Articulate Your Motivation Around Agile

Are you thinking about adopting an Agile way of working for some or all of your team's work?

If so, be aware that becoming Agile is never the goal or the end. Rather, it is a means to an end. What end are you after? What's your reason for considering a change? What vision are you pursuing, for which an Agile way of working is a good choice?

As you'll see throughout this book, Agile requires more than replacing processes and practices. Is your vision compelling enough that you're willing to start making fundamentally different choices in terms of engaging people and managing work?

The previous section mentioned several outcomes that justify using Agile. Before you continue reading this book, be clear on your top outcomes or reasons for adopting Agile. They must be real, specific, compelling reasons that matter to the organization (two common ones that do not meet these criteria: "We can always improve" and "The world is moving to Agile, we have to keep up"). If you start mobilizing people to change their way of working — even if it's the best decision you make this decade — be ready to explain why and make a compelling case.

Intrigued about Agile's potential for your team and business? In chapter 2 we'll take the next step along the pathway: clarifying what Agile actually is and thereby understanding whether and how it can help you fulfill your vision.

Chapter 2
Consider How Agile Differs from Your Current Way of Working

Tactics

Take a moment to reflect on the following question: How does your team produce results?

Chances are, your answers focus on the following **tactics**. To illustrate them, the text in parentheses provides examples from how my family doctor would answer the question about his clinic:

+ **Process or workflow**: what happens first, second, and so on (patients check in with the receptionist; she calls each patient into an available room in order of arrival; after I finish seeing a patient, I make notes in their file)

✦ **Procedures or practices**: certain actions or sequences done at specific times for specific purposes (the receptionist will have the patient's file waiting for me by the door to the examination room; I wash my hands before entering)

✦ **Roles**: who performs certain actions (I am the only person who can sign a referral to a specialist)

✦ **Meetings or touchpoints**: when the team interacts and for what purpose (we have a staff meeting every Friday afternoon to review next week's schedule)

✦ **Artifacts**: documents and other things produced in the course of the work (we keep one folder per patient, containing all my notes and their test results)

Now, let's turn our attention to Agile. More and more people are familiar with it, either from personal experience or from their colleagues in technology. Ask them to explain how Agile teams work, and you're likely to hear something like the following:

"The teams are cross-functional, meaning they have developers and testers and everyone else they need. They capture their work as 'user stories,' estimate the effort using 'story points,' and keep them in a prioritized list called a 'backlog.' A person called 'the product owner' manages the backlog. They work in two-week cycles called 'sprints'; at the beginning of each sprint, they commit to delivering several of the top items from the backlog. Every day at the same time, they have a short 'standup' meeting to talk about what they're doing and about impediments. At the end of each sprint, they demo their work to the product owner, and then they do a quick lessons-learned exercise called a 'retrospective.' There's usually someone called a 'Scrum Master' who helps remove impediments and leads the meetings."

This description is also all about tactics. Even though it's a true account of many Agile implementations, it only scratches the surface. Why? Because all those **practices, meetings, processes, artifacts, and roles don't actually matter**. The important part of a way of working is people's mind-set: their principles, values, and beliefs. These elements connect the "why" of the work and its "how." Let's define and examine the Agile mind-set, and see how its choices differ from traditional mind-sets.

SUPPLEMENTARY RESOURCE: Download the printable "Intentional Mind-Set Poster" from the book's companion website, **AgileForNonSoftwareTeams.com**.

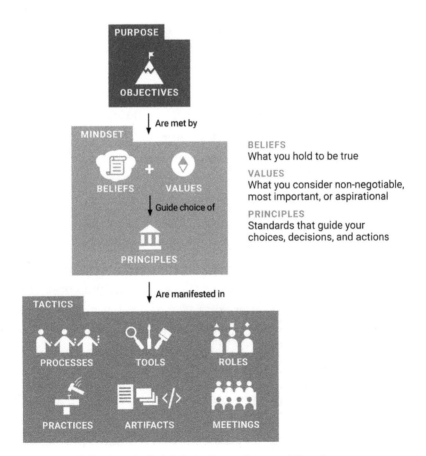

Mind-set: Bridging the why and the how

Choice-Making

We'll start unpacking the Agile mind-set at the level that gives rise to tactics: **principles**. Which principles do people employ — how do they choose, decide, and act — when working in an Agile way?

In Agile, teams are the primary working unit. They are small and laser-focused on creating products or services that matter; they deliver that value gradually and frequently to customers with whom they forge collaborative relationships. They trace everything they do to outcomes of value to the customers or to their own organization. That usually requires them to be cross-functional or multidisciplinary — having the entire range of needed skills and knowledge present in the team — even if members formally report into different functions. If the team can't be structured this way, the members at least strive for frequent collaboration with people in the organization who can help them produce and deliver value.

In terms of process, Agile teams obsess over finishing what they start so they may deliver value without delay. They always focus on the next most important task, favoring progress over perfection; while they keep the big picture (of outcomes) in mind, they plan frequently, in small bursts. They decompose work items into small pieces, and only take on small amounts of work at a time, to ensure a reliable flow of value delivery. Having a bias for action, Agile practitioners permit themselves to move forward despite uncertainty and limited knowledge.

To increase their effectiveness — to do more of the right and less of the wrong, and to get bad news early — Agile teams seek and consider feedback assiduously. They pay attention to efficiency, but only after they're sure of their effectiveness. They take extra care in sequencing their work items and executing on them so that making changes, both during the work and after the deliverable is presumably "done," is affordable.

Agile teams are tight. They congregate frequently to plan, review, and reflect together. Their meetings are collaborative, consensual, and psychologically safe. They are transparent about their work and visualize it in ways that give them full control over its flow. They carry it out with a healthy balance of collaboration, solo work, and hand-offs. Teams have sizable autonomy in terms of how they get work done, and self-organize to maximize value delivery, learning, and team growth. If they have designated leaders, those leaders are facilitative, supportive enablers, not taskmasters. Agile teams are not islands, though; they connect to the rest of the organization through their leaders and direct ties with their stakeholders.

This is Agile — without jargon, software-isms, frameworks, tools, or so-called "best practices." Compare any two great Agile teams, and you'll find they both adhere to these principles, although they may manifest them differently.

If you think about Agile at this level, you might find greater applicability to your situation. If you choose to adopt it, starting with the principles will increase your flexibility in designing workflows, structures, and management systems that truly fit your needs. If you discuss Agile with others on this level, instead of as a "how to do it" description (or prescription), it will be much easier to get them on board. Chapter 7 illuminates and expands enough on the whirlwind description given above for you to design and start using your own Agile way of working.

Nick Heling, Content Marketing Agile Coach, Red Hat:
"I wish I had done more to explain Agile without saying Scrum or Kanban or using any other jargon early on. I have had to work to uncouple the ideas of Agility from the prescribed practices."

Before you continue reading, take a moment to reflect on the principles that guide *your team*. You might need a few minutes; most people are not used to pondering this idea.

Whether your analysis yields an overlap with the Agile principles or not, let's see where those principles come from. After all, neither set of principles got picked out of thin air.

Values

Recall the beginning of the last project or initiative you were involved in. Chances are, one of the first questions people discussed was, "What is the purpose of this project?" It is basic practice in business to talk about purpose, objectives, goals, mission, or vision: *Why* do the work? What difference will it make? This discussion should, and often does, cover objectives, success criteria, constraints, and other parameters.

The team, managers, and sponsors ought to ponder another powerful question. Yet this one, unfortunately, rarely gets raised. Here are different ways of phrasing it:

"As we work, what should we optimize for?"

"What should we constantly aspire to as we do the work?"

"What aspect of delivering results is non-negotiable?"

"What are the most important parameters for getting this work done?"

"What kinds of choices should we make to maximize our chances of success?"

These questions elicit an articulation of your *values*: what's important to you. Both in plain English and in business-speak, values tend to encompass such matters as integrity, truthfulness, and inclusivity. These values drive how people engage as human beings, but don't provide enough guidance for producing results. Instead, you need to expand your attention beyond the people to the deliverable (whether product, service, one-off, or something else), the work that goes into producing it, and its customers (the entities who will benefit from it).

A value every organization and department has is "stay in business." This value is enough to keep many people predictably busy, doing such tasks as handling customer complaints, upgrading infrastructure that no longer receives technical support, and reviewing vendors' proposals for legal risks.

Other values, however, are far less obvious because they are based in choice. The choice is usually up to executives and depends on many factors. While I can't know what your executives value in your work, there's a good likelihood that the top values are these:

GETTING DELIVERABLES RIGHT THE FIRST TIME: The recipients of deliverables, along with the workers who make them, ought to understand each deliverable well enough for the workers to create it in a single, efficient pass. Changes to the work ought to be minimal, done early, and controlled closely.

Examples of work where this should be a top value:

+ Rolling out employee salary updates

+ Announcing (in a store) a deep discount on select items

+ Paying the government the correct amount of taxes

While in all cases it's possible to correct mistakes and change decisions afterward, avoiding that is better for all involved.

FOLLOWING INDUSTRY STANDARDS: Use standardized processes and industry best practices to produce the results right every time. (And if your work is unique, make your own standard operating procedures.) The process and practices should guarantee correct execution regardless of who does the work, as long as they have the necessary skills.

Examples of work where this should be a top value:

+ Conducting clinical trials

+ Flying airplanes

+ Constructing office buildings

In all these, there's both room and need for human judgment, but process and procedures should come first to ensure consistency, predictability, and safety.

DELIVERING RESULTS BY A CERTAIN TIME FRAME AND/OR WITHIN A CERTAIN BUDGET: Associate successful completion with delivery by some dates and/or with minimizing expense (including labor costs).

This value may be critical in the context of large work such as projects and initiatives. Examples of that include:

+ Replacing crumbling highways

+ Upgrading information systems to comply with new laws and regulations

+ Hosting an international conference

This value may also be critical to operational ("business as usual") work. Examples of that include:

+ Delivering customers' food orders

+ Filing (in a publicly traded company) the quarterly report

+ Adding new employees to the company's payroll and benefits program

Agile has revolutionized the world of work because it offers a fundamentally different set of choices. Here are its four values:

DELIVERING VALUE EARLY AND OFTEN: Instead of delivering value to the customer when the work is complete (whenever that happens to be), deliver portions of the value incrementally over time, preferably often.

Examples of work where this value helps improve business outcomes, and (in italics) how this value might manifest itself in the way of working:

+ Building a collaborative space for a team that's currently spread out. *Choose an empty area, supply folding tables and power bars, and let the team move in. Roll in some whiteboards and a TV. Install proper desks soon thereafter.*

+ Analyzing sales conversion data to identify improvement opportunities. *Start by analyzing simple metrics in Excel, looking for low-hanging fruit. Next, use advanced statistics to identify patterns and outliers. Then listen to a sample of recorded conversations by sales agents.*

In both of these examples, the recipients of the deliverables can start benefiting from them early, even though what they receive isn't the full solution yet.

ADAPTATION: Make changes easy, cheap, and drama-free. As work proceeds, there might be proactive or reactive changes to make to the product, whether it's a one-off or the subject of long-term investment: expansion, basic maintenance, making it more efficient or general, correcting bad decisions, and so on. The process might require changing as well, if it's not working reliably or conditions change. When you're adaptive, you still exhibit commitment and accountability toward certain goals, *and* you recalibrate them when that's necessary or worthwhile.

Examples of work where this value helps improve business outcomes, and how this value might manifest itself in the way of working:

+ Designing a graphic ad. *Start with a rough pencil-and-paper sketch; review with stakeholders; iterate. Incorporate real but not necessarily final texts; review; iterate. Design it in the proper software without worrying about fonts and colors; review; iterate. Finalize the design and texts.*

+ Hiring a consultant. *Start with a general understanding of the work to be done, the nature of deliverables, the dates, and the financials. Then review the legalities and what-ifs in bullet-point form to ensure there's no fundamental disagreement or misunderstandings. Finally, write a proper contract.*

In these examples, the deliverable has a higher likelihood to fit its intended purpose, and risks are addressed early.

CUSTOMER COLLABORATION: Let the delivery team collaborate with their customers, customer proxies, users, and stakeholders – both internal and external people — to determine outcomes and deliverables that move all parties forward.

In the simplest case, there will be a single obvious customer/user or several similar ones. For example, the small accounting firm my company employs has a collaborative relationship with us. We strive to make each other's work easier; they understand our business and are always there to answer questions; we treat each other fairly, and have never had to fall back on the contract. As their customer, I know my firm is in good hands from an accounting standpoint.

Your customers may be internal to your organization, working in separate functions or groups. In most non-Agile organizations, the relationship with them would be formal, involving hand-offs, many assumptions, and potential for negativity. Looking at the above examples again, Facilities personnel may build a space for a software team based on a specification, without ever talking to a single programmer or tester who would use the space. Or the Creative department may have its graphic designers work from requirements or briefs, then meet stakeholders only to verify conformance to those requirements or to seek approval. Now consider how much fitter for purpose the team space or the graphic ad could be if its recipients were involved throughout the process as partners, discussing ideas and developing options with the delivery team.

Even when the relationship between delivery and customer is neither formal nor negative, it's often characterized by a "let specialists do their thing" attitude. No matter how professional the specialists are, collaboration can guide their choices in good directions. For example, if HR is tasked with upgrading the organization's performance management scheme, collaborating with various functional managers may yield a scheme that incorporates the managers' perspectives — not only HR's — on positive behaviors and problematic ones. Or, Marketing can design a campaign in collaboration with several other departments to make sure they're promoting all the right things and not making any false promises. In these examples, groups that might otherwise have done "their parts" ensure, on an ongoing basis, that their parts align to make an effective whole.

If customers or users are external or numerous, and if the delivery team has no easy access to them, a proxy — who collaborates with the delivery team — may be a pragmatic compromise.

PUTTING PEOPLE FIRST: Enable people to bring their best selves to work in service of the outcomes. Treat customers, staff, and management as you would want to be treated. Allow self-organizing, collaborative teams to grow, and design a way of working that suits their situation, instead of force-fitting them to a standard process.

Examples of work where this value helps improve business outcomes, and how this value might manifest itself in the way of working:

+ Designing the company's new office. *Understand what individuals and teams need in order to be effective and engaged. Review early designs with them and consider their feedback. Allow them to choose where they'll sit.*

+ Managing people. *Allow parents of infants to bring the children to work.*[1] *Give people feedback and discuss objectives and challenges, frequently, instead of as part of a formal annual procedure.*

+ Processing insurance claims. *Pay out straightforward claims faster and with less red tape than complicated ones.*[2]

+ Accounting. *Pay small suppliers' invoices earlier than the payment terms allow.*

In these examples, replacing otherwise transactional exchanges with human-centered interactions increases positive engagement, deepens trust, and fosters goodwill, all of which in turn increase the organization's resilience and flexibility.

Perhaps as you read my explanations of the four Agile values, you were thinking them reasonable or obvious. They are certainly not obscure; in fact, entire bodies of knowledge have formed around each of them in isolation. "People first" aligns with modern organizational cultures and leadership styles. Customer involvement is increasingly becoming the norm, especially since the advent of the Internet and smartphones. The ideas of "delivering value" and making a difference to customers, rather than merely acting on requirements, are becoming commonplace in business. Adaptation and "no more big bang" are now seen as key to survival in today's fast-moving world.

Does that mean we should no longer care about dates and costs, ignore established standards, and always tell our customers, "You'll get it when it's ready?" Not at all. The values we choose are high-level preferences, and the key word here is "choose." For instance, take two values — dates and adaptation — and imagine your team has some large-scale work to do. If an expectation of a completion date accompanies the work, is delivering on that date the most important factor for success? What if, along the way, the understanding of the deliverable changes or complications arise, jeopardizing the date? What if you assume, going in, that such changes or complications are likely?

In some situations the choice between values is obvious. In *many* others, it must be deliberate, and if people (team, management, customers, stakeholders) don't make it, their results may fall short of accomplishing their intended outcome. For example, many people manage *all* their work as if it's date-constrained, even though only *some* of it truly is, thus leaving themselves little freedom of movement.* Or, teams work hard to perfect deliverables, rarely asking whether an earlier good-enough or incremental delivery is preferable. Agile has brought the matter of values and intentionality to the forefront, and the question for you is: For some or all of your work, would optimizing for its four values help you accomplish better outcomes?

---

* Sometimes, managers put dates on work as a way to spur people into action and later hold them accountable. While some workers find this mechanism helps them, I think it's the wrong solution to a misdiagnosed problem. Another solution, which helps organizations become healthier and more resilient, is to articulate the work's outcome and allow workers freedom to move within meaningful, justifiable, prioritized parameters (which might include dates).

While you can choose to adhere to only one or two of the four values, "the Agile package" is extra powerful because each of these particular values also reinforces the others. This holistic value system replaces contractual, transactional, vendor-buyer, and producer-consumer relationships between two mistrusting sides with relationships that yield outcomes of value to all partners. It replaces an obsession over costs, schedules, compliance, and efficiencies with an obsession over problems, needs, and goals worth addressing. To repeat a previous point, the key to success is to truly prize the Agile values over the other ones; that while you still care about traditional matters (such as efficiency and predictability), your default stance is to care *more* about the other choices (such as customer delight), and act accordingly.

Take, for instance, the matter of writing and publishing books. Self-publishing has become very popular, but not only due to practicality, accessibility, and higher author royalties. The traditional publisher's way of working adheres to that first set of values: authors submit proposals, publishers set deadlines, editors correct and improve authors' texts, and designers create covers with minimal author consultation, and all this is done within a standard, rigid process. In self-publishing, by contrast, the author is free to choose a different set of values by which to work. As an author, I believe (also based on my two earlier books) that working according to the Agile values would accomplish my outcomes better than traditional publishing could. I don't follow a standard process, and I can afford not to worry about the publication date and my costs, even though I keep them within reasonable ranges. Here is what this scenario looked like, six months into the writing process:

- ✦ Early and frequent value delivery: I am early to market with the electronic format of this book; the hard copy will come four months later, and the audiobook (if I decide to make it) sometime later. Readers who want the book early don't have to wait for all editions to come out at the same time, and I can distribute my workload and expenses.

✦ Customer collaboration: I've involved more than 30 people through research interviews and feedback (both early-stage and later). Later, my designers and I iterated over the book's visual appearance, instead of the designers' doing their work in isolation.

✦ Adaptation: I asked for lots of feedback on my early assumptions and intents. Authoring on the Leanpub platform, sending new sections and chapters to readers is a matter of minutes. Working only on the e-book's text most of the time, I can easily change anything.

✦ People-first: every interaction I've had came from a place of respect, trust, and collaboration. I've reengaged the same professionals who helped with my previous books, and I have a fair contract and customized workflow with each one.

Beliefs

We've looked at two of the three elements of mind-set: principles and values. It bears repeating that they are choices; for instance, you can *choose* to work adaptively, or you can *choose* to maximize predictability. You can *choose* to deliver value gradually, or you can *choose* to deliver results only once, at the end.

The third element of a mind-set is beliefs: fundamental assumptions about individuals, teams, the work, and the work's customer. Beliefs give the values context and validity. However, they can be tricky: even though they sound compelling, they're only strongly held assumptions, not facts. As you read the following narrative of Agile beliefs, notice your reactions. Do you hold similar beliefs? Opposite ones? Are they always true, or true only in some situations?

PEOPLE. Folks won't bring their best selves to work if they don't feel enough psychological safety. Competent, motivated, trusted, and supported people will do good work.[3] Pragmatically, though, as human beings they will get some (or possibly many) things wrong. Even when they're right, they're not perfect, and working closely in teams enriches the outcomes that they could achieve individually. Teams may not only be smarter and more productive than the sum of their members, they may make smarter decisions than their managers (though they might need some help evolving to greatness). Teams should have autonomy, albeit with direction.

THE CUSTOMER. The most important entity is the customer, but the customer is not always right. In fact, neither the customers nor the team can have all the answers up front, nor should they (being adaptive). Moreover, even if they have a good handle on what's needed *now*, waiting too long will make those requirements go stale. The sensible thing to do, therefore, is to focus intently on what the customer needs right now, and keep options open by not committing too far into the future. Being effective first and efficient second is good for business, and what's "effective" is a matter of outcome, not of conformance to a plan.

THE WORK. If the work is *complex* or *complicated*,[4] *emergence* (or *evolution*) is a more appropriate response than planning. The best enabler of emergence is short feedback loops. Since feedback, emergence, and adaptation imply frequent change, the team must work in ways that keep the cost of change low.

Beliefs are tricky for one other reason: we humans may say we believe something, but act differently. That doesn't necessarily make us liars; more often than not, it indicates that other beliefs hold stronger for us. The same goes for values. For example, a leader may believe that teams can do great work, and still place herself as the final authority. A customer might agree that working adaptively is worthwhile, and still present a team with detailed up-front requirements because that increases their feeling of certainty. For any group of people to succeed together, their actions must align with a shared set of beliefs and values, whether it's their natural mind-set or chosen for the situation at hand.

Agility Has Many Forms Now

As you might expect, when millions of people take a shine to a new idea, that idea never stays constant. It mutates and branches. It creates a following, business models, competition, and so on. Agile is no different. On one hand, this gives you more options; on the other hand, the set of similar options may be confusing to the point of paralysis. Here are the terms you'll encounter most frequently.

agility (lowercase A) or *business agility* is exactly what the English noun communicates: the ability to change what's delivered and how it's done, easily and gracefully. It's an attribute of an organization, team, or person. Companies are interested in agility because the world of business moves fast these days. The term "agility" alone doesn't imply any specific method, structure, or operational principle.

An *agile culture* in an organization means it tolerates or welcomes ambiguity, makes viable plans despite incomplete information, and responds to changing conditions. As with "agility," there's no additional stipulation as to how this is achieved; however, saying it's a "culture" means that acting this way is natural for the organization. It's just how it is. In an analogy, I run in several 10K races every year (I have that level of "agility") but I don't think of myself as an athlete (that would be "agile culture").

Agile (capital A), to many people, is any way of working that embodies the exact values, beliefs, and principles presented in the *Manifesto for Agile Software Development*, which was penned in 2001. Many others consider ways of working "Agile" if they follow a generalization of the *Manifesto* and factor in modern insights while maintaining its spirit. This is how I think of Agile and how I describe it in this book. For instance, where the *Manifesto* talks about "working software" or "valuable software," we'd generalize to "value delivery." We also include principles in Agile that were never mentioned in the *Manifesto*, but ones the Agile community typically considers necessary to successful Agile implementations, such as psychological safety, servant leadership,* and deferring decisions to the last responsible moment.

Scrum is the best-known framework for applying the Agile mind-set. "Framework" means that it specifies certain tactics — roles, artifacts, practices, team events — and its users are expected to add to it based on context. Scrum used to be more prescriptive than it is today; some artifacts and meeting processes are no longer considered mandatory. Many people mistakenly believe Scrum's checklist is bigger than it really is, including in it such tactics as user stories and story point estimation. Scrum is so popular that many people think it is synonymous with Agile, but in fact it is only one of many forms of implementing the Agile concepts.

Lean, conceived by Toyota, is an ancestor of Agile. Similarly to Agile, it focuses on maximizing customer value in a people-first environment, and shares with Agile many principles that bring these values to life. However, there is a fundamental difference between the two. In Agile, teams assume they don't have all the answers up front; they don't know exactly what solution will delight the customer (and often assume the customer doesn't know either until they see it). A Lean organization, by contrast, already produces a well-understood solution; using Lean thinking, it optimizes the solution's quality, maximizes speed of delivery, and minimizes waste of time, effort, money, and the like. Hence Lean's popularity in areas that prize a repeatable, smooth, minimal-delay flow of value such as manufacturing and customer service.

Kanban, which also traces its ancestry to Lean, is a set of specific principles and practices for creating balance and good flow in knowl-

---

* Servant leaders create conditions that enable others to grow and do their best work; instead of relying on power or positional authority, they serve. Agile leadership subscribes to this philosophy and enriches it with concepts relevant to Agile environments. Read more on this in chapter 9.

edge and service work. Since its values and principles are congruent with most of Agile, many Agile teams incorporate some of them into their Agile methods.

Almost all the concepts I present in this book are from Agile, some are from Kanban, and a couple are from Lean. You don't need to worry about the distinctions at this point, and your context would probably not require you to choose one and reject all the others. Rather, this book will take you through a process for designing a way of working that fits your needs.

As you can see, there is more to Agile than meets the eye. What meets the eye — usually standup meetings, boards, and teams sitting together — is not a bad idea, but it's not the part that actually matters. It might seem easy to adopt Agile practices, but going through the Agile motions without a concomitant change of mind-set — actually making different choices and caring about different things — won't create any Agility and will only confuse people. Making a real change will take work and firm intent.

If you're seeing the potential, the next steps will be to discuss with your team the possibility of using Agile and to fully address their concerns. In preparation for that, read chapter 3.

SUPPLEMENTARY RESOURCE

Go to **AgileForNonSoftwareTeams.com** and download "Intentional Mind-Set Poster."

Chapter 3
Listen to Your Team's Concerns

With Agile's growing popularity, you might get the impression (and many people will actually say) that it's the right way to go. That it's the modern alternative to the "old" approaches, whose time has passed. That you ignore it at your peril.

I'm not going to tell you any of that. What I do want for you — and your management probably wants it, as well — is to increase your contribution to greater business success.

Will an Agile way of working help you do that better than your current one? Put another way, would optimizing for the Agile values and espousing the Agile beliefs — even for part of your work — lead to better outcomes? I can't say so without knowing your context, but I can tell you this: Agile has helped turn around several different kinds of work, especially the complex and ever-changing field of software development. It seems to be having similar effects on marketing and design. The world is still discovering where and how else Agile can apply, because today's business conditions are quite different than they were even one generation ago.

Starting to use Agile, even experimentally, requires changing some things (though not necessarily many). Naturally, the people experiencing the change will have concerns. Even if you're personally convinced that Agile is the way to go, your team should be ready, willing, and able to go down that road. Discuss the possibility of using Agile with the team, focusing on the "willing" part (later chapters will help with "ready" and "able"). Explain what you learned from the first two chapters, or ask the team to read them. Articulate what you think Agile can help the team accomplish, and what problems or deficiencies it can alleviate. Focus on its approach and choice-making, not on what the process will look like (which isn't known yet anyway — that's in chapter 8). Listen to their concerns with empathy and respect, be genuine and transparent, and seek helpful responses together. If they have unaddressed concerns and you skip this step, your chances of success with Agile will unfortunately be very low. This chapter lists common concerns and how I would address them.

Isn't Agile Just for IT? How Is Adopting a Way of Working that Software Developers Use Relevant for Us?

It is true that Agile grew up and remains most popular in software development and IT. However, its practices and techniques aren't the source of its success; the mind-set that drives them is. In other words, it's the particular values (what people care about the most), beliefs (their biggest assumptions), and principles (how they make choices) that create Agility, not their particular roles, artifacts, and meetings. This mind-set has wide applicability outside software development, though there are fewer examples of it at this point (you can read several in the appendix). While I don't think Agile applies to all pursuits, it might well apply to your work or to portions of it. In chapter 4, you'll perform a brief analysis to determine that.

We Do Operational Work, Not Product Development

Agile is ideal for nonroutine work that involves complexity, change, and ambiguity and that benefits from team collaboration. That doesn't mean it can't have a positive influence on work that is less complex and dynamic than that (and I assume yours is not trivial). You might also find that applying a subset of the principles to a subset of your work would help you produce better outcomes and even enjoy the work more.

We Already Follow Industry Best Practices, so Why Should We Change Anything?

For decades, software development and IT organizations *said the same thing.* There were standard methodologies and practices, all based on classical management approaches, that presumed to guarantee success if executed correctly. With no shortage of smarts and good intents, the results often fell short of success. It took many disenchanted practitioners and managers, who dared to try something different, to realize that changing their ways of working could improve results. And it took several more years of trying, understanding, and generalizing the ideas before executives realized there was something real here. The same might happen to you. Here are two other examples of finding better alternatives to industry norms:

+ Having an annual budget is a management staple that drives much of the action in many organizations. Some very large organizations are realizing outsized improvements to the bottom line, and experiencing greater agility, by using quarterly or rolling budgets and adjusting their management systems accordingly.[1]

✦ The annual performance review cycle, with bonuses and salary increases tied to performance per expectations, has been a "best practice" for decades. Many organizations (especially those that cultivate a human-centered culture) have realized that its disadvantages far outweigh its benefits, and have replaced it with other means of supporting employee growth.

Has Agile Been Tried Before for My Kind of Work?

As the title of the book implies, it casts a wide net. For readers in marketing, design, and HR, the answer would be "yes, *and* the demand is growing." In other functions, the answer would be "yes, but less so." In specialized departments and business units, it's hard to know but the answer is probably "rarely." That does not make it wrong; we're in the early days of Agile outside of software, and thus there's little data to prove or guarantee its fit. As for getting ideas for your implementation, resist the temptation to copy what other people have done, which isn't a winning strategy. This book will guide you in designing your way of working without reliance on anyone else's solutions.

We Can't Change Our Methods Because of Regulatory Compliance Requirements

Compliance requirements rarely force organizations to work a single way. Their purpose is to maximize safety and confidence and also to reduce certain risks; organizations accomplish that by proving that their decision-making and execution protocols are reliable and safe, and by demonstrating that they actually follow them. There is nothing inherent to Agile that makes it noncompliant. When you design your way of working in chapter 8, verify that your choices conform to the requirements you face (for example, you produce certain documents and artifacts as part of the workflow). A couple of conversations with the Legal department may be all it takes to ensure compliance.

What If Agile Applies to Only a Portion of Our Work?

If Agile can improve your outcomes for that portion of the work, apply it there. Don't worry about the rest of your work, although Agile might give you ideas for smaller improvements there. (By the way, that's also the case in software development, where Agile grew up: while it's well suited for substantial parts of that work, other parts of it benefit more from Lean concepts.)

Some of the Agile Values Will Not Be Welcome Here

Some business settings have evolved in ways that are antithetical to certain Agile values. For instance, the "publish or perish," first-author paradigm in academic research does not encourage full-partnership collaboration. Similarly, entire departments exist to protect their organizations from risk (such as legal or commercial risk), and their ways of working may be far removed from the people-before-process and customer collaboration Agile priorities. In some organizations, non-Agile values and principles are so ingrained they are said to be "in their DNA."

Yet, I believe these situations are more the exception than the rule. If you feel some of the Agile values would not be welcome in your organization, try to figure out why. Is it due to the nature of the work or the business landscape? Is it an intentional cultural setting that you can trace back to a founder? Is it due to a problem that occurred long ago, and the solution still exists even though the problem won't recur? Is it due to habits and standards people brought over from their previous organizations? Or did it just get to be this way over the years, one step at a time? Your analysis might show you a way forward, though it may not be easy, requiring people with enough will and influence to change it.

I am helping an IT department at a large services firm. All the managers I talk to are loving Agile and its potential, and I can tell it's a great fit and will help them control some of the chaos. And still, every other conversation used to dead-end with, "...but we can't ever be adaptive. The way Finance works, we must know everything that a project will include, and estimate every little thing." With my support, they have started collaborating with Finance on a budgeting approach both parties can live with. That will take more time and support, and skepticism is rife, but the managers will overcome this challenge just as those in many other companies have.

We Are Not Empowered to Make Decisions; We Always React to Others' Requirements

As organizations evolve, functions and departments appear, followed by teams. To handle growth in personnel and business, managers are added. Managers have specific accountabilities and objectives with respect to their portions of the organizations. They coordinate needs and deliverables with each other to achieve business results.

This is how businesses work... in theory. In the real world, several dynamics play out. Some groups become order-takers while others lead initiatives. Personalities and relationships determine who will actually work with whom. Norms and attitudes determine which behaviors are welcome, acceptable, or frowned upon. Even if the org chart remains unchanged, all the above shifts over time as people leave and others join.

The upshot? The way your organization currently acts may not be optimal for it, and is certainly not the only possible way. If you're reactive and not empowered to do much, that *can* change, and the change might be beneficial enough to become the new way. It might take time, many little wins, an influential supporter, or a change in management, but it's possible.

If We Feel We're Already Working in an Agile Way, Will We Have to Change Anything?

While this book is for people who are starting out with non-software Agile, chances are some readers already enjoy good Agility (perhaps without thinking of it as such). If your team adapts easily to changing requests; engages in healthy ways with customers, users, and stakeholders; and regularly finishes meaningful deliverables together, good for you! The remainder of the book should provide inspiration, ideas, and references for additional improvements.

What If There Are Practices We Can't Do, or Can't Find Equivalents for?

This book will show you how to design your methods without imitating other people's practices. As I say several different ways in this book, "rolling out practices" is not a winning strategy, so we're not going to worry about that. And if some Agile principles don't seem relevant to your work, you can safely ignore them.

If Our Company Is Pursuing an Agile Transformation, Shouldn't We Just Have the Same Process as Everybody? Shouldn't There Be a Company Standard?

Many factors contribute to the success of an Agile transformation, but having a standard process or methodology isn't one of them. In fact, putting process before people is a distinctly *unAgile* value, as explained in chapter 2. After all, people across the company are different, have different needs, and do different kinds of work, so why would the same process apply to them? What you *do* need in an agile organization (and yours may need years to get there) is an empowering culture of customer and outcome orientation, cross-team collaboration, value delivery, and adaptation. As long as teams build strong habits around this value system, their tactics don't have to be identical. If you have teams that work on interdependent parts of the same product, they'll probably benefit from planning and reviewing both progress and feedback together, but the rest is up to them.

Many people worry that if teams don't use similar methods, it will be hard to manage the overall organization and to move people between teams. Even if these assumptions are true (which I doubt), the biggest challenge of Agile transformations is getting to the empowering culture and building the habits. And to do that, the best approach I know is to design your own methods to fit your particular context within an intentional, Agile-oriented organizational value system. The point is not for you to create a silo, but to get started, learn, see what works and what Agile takes, and improve over time. If you ever harmonize teams' methods, do it only after they've become Agile, and make the common process as simple as possible.

We're Already Too Busy; We Don't Need More Meetings

From the outside, it might seem that Agile teams are always in meetings, leaving little time for actual work. They meet because of their belief that they are stronger together, and one way they implement "together" is through collaborative meetings. If you work in a team, and if collaboration is a good idea for you, you should allow the team opportunities to work collaboratively. Meetings are not the only choice. And meetings that are muted, boring, and nonparticipative are a really bad choice.

Agile Seems to Have a High Administrative Overhead

Similarly to the concern about many meetings, Agile projects sometimes give the impression of requiring a lot of bureaucracy and administration, for example in keeping track of many small tasks or preparing for demo meetings. Some of that overhead is a result of the chosen Agile framework, but the rest is inherent to Agile and explained by two choices made there. One is Agile's favoring of working with small tasks, which maximizes flexibility and reliability, but results in having more items to manage than if everything were big. The other choice is Agile's favoring of transparency and collaboration, which gives everyone regular visibility into everything, whereas in non-Agile work, team members aren't privy to all information. This concern is another example of the point made in chapter 1: every way of working has pros and cons.

What If It Doesn't Work Out?

You might give Agile an honest try but struggle to make it real. You might make it real, only to realize it's not a great fit for you. For these and other reasons, I suggest (at the beginning of the next chapter) to treat it as an experiment. Make it safe and easy to undo, with no repercussions; for instance, don't change titles, reporting lines, compensation, or performance standards. And if it doesn't work out, it will still give rise to valuable conversations about the team's way of working, so squeeze every bit of learning out of it.

It's normal to have concerns about change, and it's important to discuss them openly. The Agile change is substantial enough that you must consider both what it would accomplish and how it could be problematic. It's okay to decide that Agile is not for you if you are really convinced that its mindset is not what you need to succeed. It's *not okay* to write it off because of concerns with practices, such as "we don't have anyone who could be a product owner," "we can't do automated testing," or "it's too many meetings." If the Agile narrative resonates with you, the values seem promising, and the principles sound sensible, you can make it work *your way*. If you're curious or excited about the potential and feeling up to experimenting with Agile, keep reading: the next chapter will help you decide where to try it out first.

Chapter 4
Determine Where You'll Try Agile for the First Time

When you set out to establish an Agile way of working, it's impossible to know how it might turn out. It's a complex matter, heavily dependent on its participants, and to succeed they must feel psychologically safe and collaborate with each other. If these statements sound familiar, that's because they are lifted straight from the Agile beliefs and values. As such, adopting such a way of working is itself best done in an Agile manner: gradually, iteratively, in a series of *experiments*.

Approaching the Agile journey as experiments rather than as one-and-done doesn't mean it requires any less commitment. It's still a change, and you still need to articulate its objectives, rationale, time

frame, and scope. However, taking the experimentation approach —
without presupposing success — will be authentic, because you can't
really know that it would succeed. You'll also find it easier to get others
on board, as people are generally more open to *trying* something different than to going along with definitive, hard-to-undo changes. No less
importantly, this approach will take some pressure off you.

You might need several experiments, because it's hard to get Agile
right, especially when people are not used to its concepts. Therefore, don't
start with big bets, but don't apply it to minor work, either. Whether it
succeeds or fails, each experiment should teach you and your team a lot.
It's fine to start by applying a simple Agile way of working to a subset of
the work with a subset of the staff. It is also possible to go whole-hog,
switching your entire operating model to an Agile one; however, if you're
in a field that's not used to Agile, and you're only using this book and not
situational, real-time expert advice, that might be too risky.

This chapter takes you through a process that I use in Agile readi-
ness assessments to determine the work on which you'll run your first
Agile experiment.

Inventory All the Work You Do

Given that Agile focuses on both the work and how it matters, the
first step is to answer these questions:

1. What products, services, or solutions do you provide?

2. What are your other major responsibilities or activities?

3. What work goes into (1) and (2)?

Even if you think these questions are easy, write the answers down.
If the first question gives you pause — you're not used to thinking of your
work this way — try starting with the second question. (For instance,
doing this exercise for 3P Vantage, my own business, question 1 is easy
to answer with "mind-set coaching," "private courses," "books," and

so on. Question 2 adds "marketing," "business development," "professional development," and more.) Unless you're converting your entire operation to Agile, focus questions 1 and 2 only on those areas that have a chance of making it to the first Agile experiment.

Take your time with this exercise; go back and forth between all three questions until you have a clear picture of the most interesting parts of your work. For an example of how the answers might evolve, imagine a large corporation's Learning & Development group starting with the first question and giving an easy, obvious answer: "training." Going to question 3, they'll include: bring external trainers on board and add their courses to our roster, maintain course information in the learning management system, arrange training space, sign up learners, deliver courses, solicit and process learner feedback, and support internal trainers. Looking at the list, they might replace the vague first answer, "training," with "maintain catalog of internally offered courses" and "scheduled classes," and perhaps some other services and solutions as well.

If you realize that certain products, services, or solutions have variants that require very different work, separate them. In the above example, "scheduled classes" is really two services, "requested sessions" and "open-enrollment sessions," since hosting a class for a group that's asked for it is much simpler than offering a quarterly class and having to fill it up with enough students every time.

Important: If your people only do a piece of a bigger product, and the piece doesn't deliver customer or business value on its own, doing Agile strictly within your team will have very limited business effect. You may have to expand the scope of some of the deliverables and the work. Consider doing the exercise together with the colleagues who produce the other pieces and eventually forming a cross-functional team. If this is not in the cards, at least involve them (and their managers) early in the thinking process and rely on personal relationships to build bridges for collaboration.

Example: The Marketing department of a media company spends most of its time promoting the company's many new and multiseason shows (and, to a lesser extent, the brand itself). Marketing a show is usually time-bounded and comprises many tasks, including:

+ Develop campaign strategy and timelines.

+ Write a "creative brief" guiding the Creative department on which graphic assets to make.

+ Write content.

+ When the campaign is active, get the right files to the right channels at the right time, post to social media, and monitor the conversations there.

Notice how Marketing depends on Creative for viable campaigns, while Creative needs Marketing for their deliverables to matter. In fact, strategy development also requires Research input so that decisions are as data-driven as possible. Thus, Marketing could team up with both Creative and Research on this exercise. Looking at the work that goes into building campaigns, the second task wouldn't be a hand-off one but a team-level one, "create graphic assets." Marketing would probably keep approaching campaign *operation* as a separate activity, because the skill set, timeline, and focus it requires are very different.

Narrow Down the List

Narrow down your list of answers to questions 1 and 2 to those undertakings that require a meaningful chunk of the team's effort. That will make your Agile experiment *real*, so you will learn a lot from it and potentially have a good effect on business outcomes.

Now, turn your attention to the work that goes into each of those undertakings. Each item on the work list probably falls into one of these general categories:

- ✦ Development: the gradual creation of a new offering or enhancement to an existing one. Some of it might be executed in projects. Development work may also be discretionary, done if time and money allow. (Example: designing a new course.)

- ✦ Production: the making of something, usually many times over, from blueprints or specifications. (Example: printing materials for a scheduled course session.)

- ✦ Business as usual (BAU), also called operational or mission-critical work: the performance of tasks required for the organization's ongoing operation. Some of these tasks might be cyclical, occurring at regular intervals. Some BAU might be production work. (Example: scheduling, filling, and teaching a quarterly open-enrollment session of an established course.)

- ✦ Support: addressing issues that people encounter when using your work product. Much of it likely requires quick turnaround. (Example: refunding a student who cancelled early enough.)

Most likely, each undertaking requires work from each category. You might want to narrow the list down to those that have a relatively large development component, since that's where Agile particularly shines. That doesn't mean it's suited uniquely to development, though.*

If your list still has several items, choose the first target for Agile. Later on in this chapter, you'll analyze the values and beliefs around it to confirm Agile's relevance. If you're going with several targets, you'll probably need to analyze them separately: their different needs, complexities, and commitments might justify different ways of working, even if

---

* Available literature and training on Agile might give you the impression that it's only for development. That's because it focuses almost exclusively on software teams, which typically work on single large products and mostly engage in development. What production they do is mostly automated, there's little BAU, and other departments usually handle support. This arrangement is due to the traditional function-orientation of organizational structures, to the high number of people required for the development of software, and to the disruptive effect of unpredictable support work on the focus needed for development.

they are all done by the same people. Given the learning curve, I recommend starting with only one target; that will already teach you a lot.

Your Agile experiment will require a cross-functional team that can turn out finished goods — not only pieces — and that can in fact act as a team. They might have to renegotiate some other obligations, or rearrange their schedules, to have enough opportunities for teamwork. You probably already have an idea who those team members are, but be open to the possibility that the roster may change after you dive into the actual design of their workflow (chapter 8).

> To continue the media company example, they could experiment with one cross-functional team working on one campaign. The team could schedule the same several blocks of time every week for working together on their campaign, and the rest of the time individuals would work on their other commitments. Later on, they might expand the experiment by taking on more shows or by forming additional teams.

If you decide to address several targets with two teams or more, try to minimize overlap of personnel across the teams; that will reduce some of the growing pains. For simplicity, the rest of this book's guidance refers to a single team, and you'd apply the guidance to each team separately.

Frame the Work

This step consists of a series of questions that crystallize team alignment around the work's key parameters and thereby facilitate the choosing of a suitable way of working. These questions generally form part of a process called chartering, which should take two or three hours.[1] While the answers to some of the questions might seem obvious, in my experience they always uncover twists and subtleties that have an outsized effect on the rest of the design.

I'll demonstrate these questions with answers given by a client, the Talent Acquisition team at an investment firm. This team of four is involved in the entire hiring process.

Who Are Your Customers?

Other ways to ask this: Whom do you serve? Who uses your deliverables? Who pays for them? Who benefits from your work (or loses if you don't deliver results)? Whose outcomes does your work support? The answers might include several people, entities, or groups of them. It's almost never the people who manage the work or the workers.

Later, the team will organize around creating value to those customers, so clarity is paramount. If the answer is some large, amorphous group ("the company," "management," "stakeholders"), make it more concrete. Consider identifying a few specific people, or making up "personas," who represent the group. Consider whether subsets of your customers have different needs, expectations, or constraints.

> The Talent Acquisition team said: "Our customers are hiring managers, the firm's managing directors, and every candidate we speak to (even if we don't hire them)."

What Is the Value of the Products and Deliverables to Your Customers and the Organization?

In other words, how do those products and deliverables make a difference to those specific people? It is important to distinguish the work and the deliverables from the outcomes they make possible. This is as true for BAU, support, and production as it is for development. By thinking about the outcomes — problems solved, needs addressed, goals achieved — you'll expand the space of viable ways of working. The answer(s) should briefly communicate, qualitatively or quantitatively, why the deliverables are worth the effort. There might be several answers if your products or customers are diverse. The answer(s) may be the same as the team's *mission statement*: its North Star or raison d'etre.

> "We help hiring managers invest the minimal amount of time filling a position with someone great."
>
> "We increase the firm's success and affect its culture through hiring." *(This was the team's mission statement.)*

What Does Success Look Like — for You, for Your Customers, for Your Organization?

This question makes the previous answer more concrete and tangible. When you are successful and your deliverables accomplish their intended outcomes, what will you see? Look for business and human effects, *not* features of the product or the fact that it's finished and delivered.

> "The people we hire integrate well, perform well, and stay long-term."
>
> "We don't lose good candidates through our own actions."

How Are You Constrained?

What expectations or obligations limit your freedom to move? How do external factors affect your ability to plan, execute, and finish work? Every constraint you identify will limit your options for potential ways of working, so look for natural and real constraints, rather than assumed, reasoned, or artificial ones.

> "Hiring managers' busy schedules cause an otherwise straightforward process to stretch out over a couple of weeks, which can cause us to lose candidates."
>
> "Our understanding of the work in each department is not enough to answer candidates' questions."

I'm sure you've faced all these questions before. Many professionals ask them, in one form or another, at the early stages of significant work or when launching a team. Effective leaders repeatedly weave the answers into general discourse to keep staff focused on doing work that counts. However, these questions are not enough for designing a way of working that maximizes success.

The following two questions provide the missing piece, which chapter 2 explained: values and beliefs. Take your time working through them, because these matters are neither straightforward nor a subject of everyday thinking. Write down ideas as you go along, to make developing and comparing options easier. Expect to go back and forth between the values and beliefs questions, because they work in tandem. Since this book is a linear medium, I had to put one first; I chose values, as most people I've worked with had an easier time starting with values and then going to the beliefs that explain and inform them. You might prefer instead to start with the beliefs.

Which Values Will Maximize the Chance of Success?

Other ways to ask this: As the team works, what should they optimize for? What are the top three to five values that should guide all choices? What is nonnegotiable? What is critical for their success?

Values are concepts, phrases, or expressions. You should be able to fit each value X into the templates "X is important to us" or "We care about X" or "We optimize for X" and produce a valid sentence. For instance, "delivering on schedule" and "adapting gracefully and economically to change" are values.

If the answers only capture what management told you, or what has been considered or assumed to be important so far (common examples are "meeting the deadline we're given" and "maximizing efficiency"), nothing will change about your way of working. That may not be a bad thing, but... what other values might yield better outcomes? What would you want to optimize for, but haven't yet? What different story would you like to tell? What do you want to be like? You are looking for *aspirational* values.

> Few professionals ever ponder these questions, which may lead them to keeping an underperforming way of working. And as mentioned in chapter 1, even when they *do* choose their values, their choices have pros and cons.
>
> Russ Dickerson, Hardware Engineering Director, Synapse Wireless:
>
> "We tried optimizing for costs, and that caused schedules to drag out. So we tried optimizing for utilization, keeping every engineer fully loaded. That created a ton of work in progress and nothing moved. We got better results by optimizing for time and being flexible with costs: we were getting more prototypes in, testing in parallel, adding people when necessary."

Two processes I've successfully used to elicit the team's aspirational values are:

- ✦ Ask each person to write their ideas on sticky notes, one per note. As people post their notes on a wall or whiteboard, they explain what they meant and why they think those are the right values; they also eliminate any duplication and rewrite some texts as needed. They vote on a shortlist and verify that it's coherent and appropriate.

- ✦ Prepare an inventory of 10 or more possible values.* Ask the team to add more values they consider relevant or promising. Discuss each item in the inventory and seek the team's sense of its criticality for their success. If it's not high, remove it from the inventory.

---

* You'll find many examples in chapter 2. Additional ones I use sometimes are "data quality," "innovation," "keeping the auditor/regulator happy," and "avoiding disaster."

Whichever process you use, if the resulting list has more than five values, discuss how to reduce it to the few that are truly fundamental and nonnegotiable.

Putting the values and constraints together, if you notice contradictions (which may be subtle), you'll have to prioritize them, or find ways to relax some constraints. For instance, if delivering on a certain date is mandatory or desirable, and responsiveness is *also* desirable, you must decide what comes first. If you decide that the date matters more, that will restrict how adaptive you'll realistically be. If you determine that responsiveness is critical for producing a viable result, you might end up having to renegotiate the date. Remember, pros and cons!

The Talent Acquisition team chose:

+ Great candidate experience

+ Close collaboration with both hiring manager and candidate

+ Taking a holistic, long-term view

What Do You (or Should You) Believe about the People, the Work, the Customers, the Business Landscape, and Changes?

What are your assumptions about:

+ The individuals, teams, and managers involved in doing the work? (For instance, what are their strengths? What do they need to succeed?)

+ The nature, special aspects, and complexity of the work? (For example, does it require or benefit from interdependence among workers? Can you reliably figure out the nature of your deliverables and the path toward them? Are most work items similar, or do they vary in risk and challenge? What kinds of interactions with people outside your team do they require?)

+ The expectations, tendencies, frame of mind, concerns, and delights of the people who ask for the work and benefit from it? (For instance, how easy is it for them to articulate their needs or to give feedback? Which aspects of the work matter most to them? What is the communication or collaboration with them like? How does their personal approach to work planning affect your own?)

+ The business landscape? (For example, how fast does it change, and in what ways?)

+ The kinds of changes you might want or have to make during the creation of the product/service and after it's done? (For instance, which choices are easy to undo, and which changes would effectively require you to start over?)

Unlike values, beliefs are true-sounding full sentences. For instance, "Everyone will do what's best for the company if we treat them right" and "Our customers can change their minds anytime, but everything is negotiable, especially if it's expensive" are beliefs.

A set of beliefs forms a narrative, which in turn acts as the backdrop to a team's work. Alas, few teams and leaders take the time to make their narrative explicit, as suggested here. If they did, some would discover that their colleagues hold wildly different beliefs, and thus work at cross-purposes. As an added benefit, articulating beliefs — especially in a team setting — makes it easier to examine their veracity and utility.

In addition to articulating the current narrative, identify which parts of it you'd like to question (including parts that sound like fact or accepted wisdom) and identify other beliefs you'd like to try on. As with determining the values, you're looking for a potentially different future. For example, if one of the current beliefs is "Tasks should be done by specialists," would going with "Most tasks can be done by anyone, except the very risky ones" possibly lead to better outcomes? Or if one of the beliefs is "We should do what our stake-holders want from us," could better results flow from acting as if "What our stakeholders tell us isn't always the best thing we could give them"?

> "The enemy of embracing the status quo is missed opportunity."
> ~ *Tom Diedrich*

You can elicit beliefs by simply asking the team variations on these questions:

- ✦ "What are some things we take for granted (and perhaps shouldn't)?"

- ✦ "Why do we say we value X?" (Note: you might hear "We value X because X is important," which merely redefines the word "value." Probe for justifications; for example, if you hear "We value adaptation *because* conditions can change anytime," the underlying belief is "Conditions can change anytime.")

- ✦ "What sort of things do we usually say to each other about [the work/the customers/the business landscape]?"

- ✦ "Which issues keep coming up in our work? What assumptions can explain them? What could we change?"

- ✦ "What kinds of changes do we face or regularly get surprised by?"

You can also identify beliefs by listening. Whenever the team or management discusses work, listen for statements that sound like strongly held truths, and write them down. Or, listen to commentary like "Process X is broken" or "I wish we did Y differently."

A third way to identify beliefs is to infer them. Observe people's behaviors and the choices they make; infer the assumptions that justify those choices, and articulate them to check that you got them right.

The Talent Acquisition team chose:

+ "We've been trying to hire the best people, but we really need to hire the *right* people."

+ "Potential often trumps 'hitting the ground running'."

+ "The hiring manager may not have asked all the right questions to make the right hire."

+ "We may not have a full perspective on the manager–needs–candidate triangle."

+ "The first 90 days really matter."

+ "New hires continue to trust their *recruiter* (but not HR!) beyond the hiring process."

+ "Candidates appreciate our honesty with them."

SUPPLEMENTARY RESOURCE: Download "Chartering Checklist" from the book's companion website, **AgileForNonSoftwareTeams.com**.

Examine the Results

Review both your prioritized values and constraints and the belief narrative. Now review the Agile values and beliefs explained in chapter 2. While probably not worded the same way, are the two lists wholly, or largely, congruent? Do they tell similar stories? If so, *Agile concepts are applicable to the work you've identified*, and the rest of this book will guide you in how to put them in place.

If the congruence is not complete, that might lead you to create a hybrid way of working. This situation is quite common, in fact. For instance, one of my clients, a pension fund, has had to make sweeping changes to its money management approach after a major change in federal legislation. It had to be ready by a government-imposed date *and* to be adaptive and collaborative, because the change touched every aspect of its operations in ways it had never experienced before. In other cases, customers aren't interested in frequent delivery of the emerging product, but *are* keen to inspect and adapt it as it evolves to maximize its eventual fit for purpose. Many other scenarios of partial congruence are likely. This book will help you in this case, as well.

It may also happen that your elicited values and beliefs have little or nothing in common with Agile. For example, your list of values contains only "get it right the first time," "deliver on time and on budget," and "adopt/establish standard processes." Or, your beliefs include such items as "We must nail down most choices early, because the cost of changing them later is prohibitive," "The best way to minimize errors is to supervise the staff," and "As long as each individual worker has the necessary skills and does their part right, we're good." There are indeed *many* professional pursuits where these values and assumptions are the most appropriate ones to espouse. If that's your case, this book (and Agile) are probably not for you. However, if you're intent on trying something new — if you're keen to tell a new story and optimize for different things — go back to the "Frame the Work" section and try it again.

I did that myself recently. In late 2016, I hired a studio to produce my book *The Agile Mind-Set* in audio. The studio held the aforementioned non-Agile values and beliefs, and worked accordingly. I liked the audiobook, but didn't appreciate that I had very little influence over it and that they refused to apply many of my requested changes (doing so would have reduced their profit, since we had a fixed-price contract). For my next audiobook, I chose another studio that explicitly valued great listener experience — via my full involvement in the process — over staying within the fixed price. The producer told me to assume that *everything* was changeable, and I committed to pay extra if that was the fair thing to do. Early on, we worked out a process (which was new to both of us) and adapted it as we went. Notice: with the same work and the same customer, a different mind-set led to different yet effective ways of working.

You have the motivation, you've addressed the concerns, and you know where to start applying Agile. Don't implement anything just yet; instead, read chapter 5 to understand key points about the journey that awaits you.

SUPPLEMENTARY RESOURCE

Go to **AgileForNonSoftwareTeams.com** and download "Chartering Checklist."

Chapter 5
Understand that It Will Be a Journey, and It Can Go Wrong

I wish I could say that achieving agility required only surface changes, such as colocating team members, holding daily standup meetings, and demoing work every two weeks. I can't. It would be the same as saying, "Buy a new wardrobe and dress differently, you'll be a whole new person!" *Becoming Agile* requires making deeper changes to engaging people, managing work, defining success, communicating, behaving, and so on. In that, it bears greater resemblance to emigrating to a new country and integrating into its society (which might include updating your wardrobe to fit the custom there).

That is one of the reasons the term "Agile adoption," popular in the early 2000s, has given way to the term more common now, "Agile transformation," for which the predominant metaphor is "the journey." This chapter reviews key conditions and pitfalls to consider.

Voluntary Participation

A common fallacy is that Agile is a methodology, a process, or merely a set of practices to adopt. Organizations that approach it this way are unaware of how intimately it's tied into culture, and culture is fundamentally about people. Those who struggle with Agile the most (or outright reject it) are those used to equating people with "resources" to be utilized and controlled.

Interestingly (and sadly), many organizations have a control culture without realizing it or even intending it to be that way. I recently assessed the operating model of a large IT department, and characterized their culture as "the friendliest command and control." Many of the managers and individual contributors there had been working with each other for more than a decade, and were respectful, collegial, and helpful; yet how they planned and executed work was clearly a matter of top-down labor extraction.

If you roll out new processes and practices, your team will have to execute them. After all, they are bound by an employment contract. Yet if they're not interested, they will not accomplish great results. They will nominally do the work and produce outputs, but won't care about achieving outcomes and their customers' success. To avoid this "check the box" mentality and enable everyone to bring their best selves to work, the environment must satisfy four related conditions:

+ **Psychological safety:** feeling that it's okay to speak up, offer options, ask for feedback, share bad news, make mistakes (if handled responsibly), customize, or push back[1]

✦ **Respect:** honoring each other's whole humanity, accepting their choices, and assuming they act in good faith

✦ **Trust:** assuming that people will work toward the stated shared objectives, do the best as they see it, and take responsibility when challenges occur along the way

✦ **Transparency:** having easy access to understandable information, especially to how decisions got made

I'm not aware of any work environment that fulfills all four conditions perfectly. That may even be unrealistic when people are there primarily to make a living. Nevertheless, there does seem to be some minimum threshold under which people will only engage to the extent of their job description and not to a higher standard that enables Agility. If you're sensing that your team's experience is under such a threshold, work on improving it before introducing Agile concepts. People will not want to make a change when the target is incongruent with their reality.

The Experience of Change

Every human being experiences change in a unique, personal, and contextual manner. Nevertheless, all experiences of change seem to follow a universal progression known as the Satir Change Model. When the change is team-level, the team as a whole will follow this progression, and each team member will move along his or her own curve. This is true of both personal and professional changes, as well as of voluntary and imposed changes.

Think of a significant change you recently went through. As you read the following description of the Satir model's stages, consider how they reflect or explain your experience.

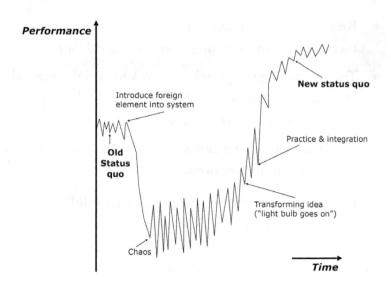

The Satir Change Model

Before the introduction of the change (*foreign element*), your performance is stable; that is the *old status quo*, popularly known as the comfort zone. When the change happens, your performance will drop precipitously: you might lack pertinent skills, react inappropriately to stimuli, and resist the change. You will spend the next period of time — ranging from minutes to months, depending on the change — in *chaos*. You will still underperform, at times less so and at other times more. At some point, you will have a *transforming idea*: the light bulb will go on in your mind as you realize the meaning of the change and appropriate responses to it. In the next phase, practice will lead to *integration* of the new skills, behaviors, expectations, and attitudes. You will eventually reach a *new status quo*, which is, you hope, better than the old status quo.

You must expect the chaos period, and prepare your team, management, and stakeholders to expect it. In software/IT teams adopting Agile (which is where we have the most data), the chaos period rarely takes less than two months, and usually takes several more. In your line of work — with fewer reference experiences, Agile experts, and lessons learned — it would probably not be shorter. During this time, your team will struggle. Competent people who successfully followed the old process now find themselves in unfamiliar territory. Their natural reaction will be to reject the change as a failure or a bad idea. If that coping strategy fails, the next natural reaction will be to think "What's wrong with me? Why am I not getting this?" Treat them gently and help them be kind to themselves: the rocky period is not a reflection on their abilities but on their being human. Have faith and tough it out — it's not easy!

Between the two stages called "chaos" and "practice and integration," an event needs to take place: having the transforming idea. In that light bulb moment, something deep changes in your understanding, self-perception, or mind-set. Typical examples of this moment in Agile transformations include:

+ Realizing that to work "iteratively and incrementally" does not mean "quick and dirty," but rather to "start with a small subset of the value, do it cleanly, and expand out"

+ Understanding that collaboration is an intentional joint effort, rather than merely working alongside peers, being helpful, or coordinating tasks

+ Leaders' recognizing that how they talk about missed expectations and commitments can make the difference between engaged and disengaged workers

The longer people take to arrive at the transforming idea, the likelier they are to experience failures and setbacks that will make them give up. However, getting the transforming idea is not a matter of serendipity or elapsed time. Allow people the space to try things out safely, reflect on their experiences, and learn from them. Make learning, at this point in time, at least as important as delivering results.

If your team members sometimes use the expression "We tried it, and it didn't work" (whatever "it" happens to be), take extra care. I hear it a lot in regard to botched or half-hearted Agile implementations; while they rarely cause serious business harm, the affected teams and managers lose interest and motivation, which makes a second attempt much harder. If you're on your first go at Agile, take it seriously and give it every chance to succeed. In particular, as the next section recommends, don't adopt "best practices" or frameworks on faith, but rather take the time to collaboratively design your own custom way of working. If you're on your second go at Agile, start by getting your team together to dig into the first attempt and learn what happened there. You might even have to replace the term "Agile" with something else that has less baggage.

Don't Start with Practices, Frameworks, or Tools

As we've seen, the mind-set is the important part of a way of working. Of course, you need to determine the other part, the tactics: process, practices, procedures, artifacts, roles, meetings, and tools. You have a few options here: implement a specific *framework*, copy someone else's tactics, or design your own. Let's review them.

A framework is a prepackaged starter solution. About a half-dozen Agile frameworks have been documented and are in wide use. For instance, if you choose the most popular one (Scrum), you'd establish three specific roles (such as "product owner"), four specific team meetings (such as "the daily Scrum," also known as "the daily standup"), several artifacts (such as the "product backlog"), and so on. You might adopt popular practices that frequently accompany Scrum but are not an official part of it, such as sizing work items using a small set of numbers drawn from the Fibonacci sequence (1, 2, 3, 5, 8, 13...). You might also install electronic tools to help you do all of the above.

I do *not* advise starting your Agile journey with a framework, despite their popularity and promises. Claiming to be universal solutions, frameworks are actually shortcuts that ignore context and deprive people of freedom and choice. Installing a framework will not bring about the culture and mind-set changes needed to support the framework. To be successful, you must start with mind-set, defining how *you* want to *be*. You must be intentional about that, instead of having a framework dictate it to you. You started down that path in chapter 4 when you articulated the values and beliefs for your first Agile target.

Copying tactics from groups who do similar work, or from your IT colleagues, may also not fit your unique context. Some tactics might come with the halo of "best practices," and you might be told that it's okay to follow them until you get the hang of Agile, and then to study the theory so you can adapt further. That model, known as Shu-Ha-Ri,[2] has *not* shown itself to be a reliable way to achieve Agility. Adopting Agile practices — even the "staples," such as task boards, sprints, stand-ups, and collaborative spaces — won't make you Agile if the heart isn't there or if the organization's mind-set trumps the Agile values. Becoming Agile is a fundamental *change in approach* (philosophy, even), and you can't achieve that kind of change using the same process for *learning skills* such as driving, playing a musical instrument, or karate.

I recommend collaborating with your team on designing their methods. This is empowering and respectful, for sure, and it's also practical for buy-in. If you go to your team with fully baked methods, they will see them as prescription or imposition, and few teams appreciate that. They will, however, appreciate a compelling vision, transparent reasons, clarity on how to continue being successful, and your ongoing support. If your first attempt at Agile stalls, rallying people for a second attempt will be hard! Read at least through chapter 8 and follow my guidance; if your analysis shows that one of the popular frameworks would fit your situation as well as a custom design would, choose among them at that point.

The Risk of Misalignment

As explained in chapter 2, beliefs (strongly held assumptions) and values (what's important or optimized for) give rise to principles (the standards for action, decision-making, and choosing among options). In turn, these three elements of mind-set give rise to tactics.

For instance, if getting your deliverables right the first time is important to you, and if you believe that you can put together a useful plan for that, it would make sense to plan your work before start-ing anything and then, when you execute, to follow your plan. Your tactics might include a project planning phase replete with detailed estimates and dependency analysis, a Gantt chart, and weekly status meetings with team leaders. This example is characteristic of classic project management.

In a counterexample, if you value adaptation, and believe that short feedback loops are a practical means for informing change, you could choose to plan and execute your work in short cycles. You might have weekly meetings to demo the team's work to stakeholders, followed by a planning meeting that takes their feedback and any new information into account. This example is characteristic of many Agile teams.

In each of these examples, the mind-set is self-consistent (the princi-ples support the values and agree with the beliefs) and is also congruent with the tactics. This alignment is important so that everyone knows how to behave and has a coherent work experience, even if the values are not the optimal choice for the desired outcomes, or if some of the beliefs turn out to be false. Your team's current tactics are probably con-gruent with their mind-set, even if they've never articulated it.

What you'll want to avoid are two forms of *misalignment*. One form is when the mind-set is incongruent with the tactics: people claim to value or believe certain things, but their actions indicate otherwise. This misalignment is common in Agile adoptions where teams replace their tactics with "Agile-looking" ones but hold on to their existing mind-set. For example, they conduct a daily "standup" meeting, but instead of being a collaborative, quick planning event for the team and by the team, they run it as a status report for the manager. Or, they don't start any work until they've received the full set of requirements with a proper sign-off.

The other form of misalignment is when people who depend on each other for success operate with different mind-sets. That can happen within teams; for instance, when some people seek collaboration, while others do their own work solo, heads-down, wearing headphones. In another common scenario, the entire team genuinely adopts the Agile mind-set, but their management and stakeholders change nothing about theirs. For example, the team might congregate every week to plan the next sprint (cycle), but its contents were predetermined for them weeks ago in a big project plan; they simply cannot be adaptive. Or, the team thrives on collaboration, but management keeps assigning tasks to individuals in a bid to maximize efficiency and "resource utilization."

These misalignments create dysfunction that affects everyone. They confuse people, who hoped to get certain results but get others. They engender disenchantment, ill will, and blame. They produce outcomes that fall short of the needed ones. You'll need to pay attention to both mind-set and tactics from day one, and see that everyone's aligned.

An Agile transformation (away from traditional and "industry standard" methods) is arguably the deepest form of organizational change a person will experience in his or her career. It is not simple, straightforward, or quick. Nor is it a guaranteed success. When you're ready to commit to the experiment, given the points raised above, proceed to chapter 6 for advice on preparations that will maximize its chances of success.

Chapter 6
Prepare for the Journey

As explained in chapter 4, it's helpful to frame the journey as a series of experiments. Expect each one to take several months; people need time to absorb and adapt new approaches, and the value and pain points of those approaches aren't always immediately apparent. This chapter reviews key preparations to make before you start the journey.

Choose a Good Time to Start

Given the duration of these experiments, choose carefully when to start. The team will need enough bandwidth for experimenting with the new ways. If they already drown in work, they will focus all their attention on the work, not on learning. (Although, if drowning in work is their regular experience, adopting Agile ways of working might soon reduce or eliminate that problem!) If they have some unallocated time, it can't be too fragmented; they will require dedicated, undistracted periods of time to have meaningful experiences. For instance, they should have sufficient, frequent, regular opportunities to meet as a team to plan, review, or reflect together.

If your team undertakes projects, either occasionally or regularly, consider starting an experiment after a big project ends. At that time, they might have more bandwidth and focus than usual. Having just finished and no longer being in the midst of action, they might feel more amenable to noticing how their way of working on that recent project helped it or hindered it. And, having time to think before the next project, they might be inclined to try the Agile approach on that next one.

If, on the other hand, your team has been working on a project for more than one-third of its expected duration, consider waiting with Agile until the project is over. This far in, on most non-Agile projects, all high-impact decisions have been made and the team merely has to execute. Changing your approach at this point will neither make much difference nor teach them much about Agile.

Get Your Manager and Stakeholders on Board

Perhaps your manager and stakeholders are already motivated, excited, and versed in Agile; perhaps they were even the ones to initiate the move. Be careful about making assumptions there: all too often, managers ask for Agile without quite realizing what they are asking for, or expect something else (usually, to make the team use Scrum tactics). Another common misunderstanding is when they assume that Agile is something you do only in your group and that it has no bearing on them ("I don't care how you execute" is a common refrain). Instead of collaborating with you, they'll merely tolerate it, as long as you deliver as usual and don't make *them* do any extra work.

To the extent possible, collaborate with your manager as you proceed along the pathway I recommend in this book. Be clear on how your proposed direction also helps your manager with his or her own accountabilities. Perhaps more importantly, discuss how managerial actions contribute to shaping the organizational system, which in turn influence team behaviors (for better or worse). Your manager's committed support will be critical, particularly around making it *safe to fail*. Nobody sets out to fail, but in the next few months, you and your team will be learning new ways, and that will involve mistakes. Making up for those mistakes and squeezing all possible learning from them will be critical for continued improvement and a healthy culture. The other common response — castigating the team and demanding accountability — will make people retreat to the perceived safety of their traditional methods and thus stop the journey dead in its tracks.

As for your stakeholders, don't assume they'll naturally go along with Agile. Educate them about it, focusing your conversations more on the values and principles than on process. Help them see for themselves how being deliberate about adaptability, frequent value delivery, and collaboration would help improve business outcomes. With each stakeholder, be sensitive to their own motivations and concerns, and lead the conversations toward shared objectives and mutual commitment. Most internal customers aren't used to being collaborative with the teams, and thus may act in familiar but unhelpful manners such as disengagement, micromanagement, or dictation.

Err on the side of overcommunicating. Expect to talk to some people more than once, as they might need some time to let the concepts sink in. Be intentional and careful even about the words you use, since ways of working involve abstract and subjective terms, which others may interpret differently than you do.

Nick Heling, Content Marketing Agile Coach, Red Hat:

"We have authored internal documents, like an Agile glossary, that help keep everyone on the same page. Sometimes people are embarrassed to ask what things mean, but if we provide resources, they can find out without having to expose their insecurity."

Assuming the Agile experiment doesn't cover all of the team's work, the members will be regularly switching between two modes. Part of the time, they'll collaborate on the experiment's work, and the rest of the time they'll perform their other tasks according to the current way of working. In such a setting, a common risk to the experiment is suffocation. (This risk is heightened if some of the Agile team members report to different managers.) Urgent non-experiment work, short-notice tasks, requests for specific team members' expertise — all these may encroach on the time and attention people can devote to their Agile team. These interferences only need to happen a few times before people start doubting the practicality of the experiment, and thereby the applicability of Agile. Discuss this risk with the other managers and stakeholders, and prepare a strategy for protecting the experiment.

Prepare the Team

Working in an Agile way will touch your team deeply. It changes the dynamics of interactions, the expectations people have from each other, and what it takes to succeed. All involved need to *want* to work and engage differently. Even if the team is willing to give it a try and the experiment is safe (chapters 3 and 4 helped you get to this point), there's no guarantee of smooth progress. In fact, several matters typically complicate Agile journeys from the get-go. As you read this list, note which ones hold in your situation:

MOTIVATION. Some team members have no problem with the status quo; by current standards, they are successful. They might say "yes" to trying something new, but deep down they wouldn't mind keeping things as they are.

INTEREST. Few people find "process" or "methodology" exciting, yet that's how most people incorrectly refer to Agile.

EMPOWERMENT. Those who realize that Agile is a mind-set for empowered teams might think it doesn't apply to them because they don't make the calls right now. And if the intent to go Agile is mandated from above, you can expect apprehension and anxiety. (Mandated Agile has a very low success rate.)

LANGUAGE. Some Agile-related words have interpretations and associations that may turn people off. For example, in many Agile implementations, leaders refer to the meetings as "ceremonies" or "rituals," words that don't usually communicate a collaborative, positive, empowered team experience. Words may also have baggage in your particular context. At one client, I was told that "process" meant "They tell me what to do, I do it, then I send it for approval," which is quite different from how I use the term. (We decided to use "workflow" instead.)

THE EXPERIENCE OF CHANGE. You might have IT colleagues who have experienced their own Agile journey. Your team members will probably talk to them, and whether their colleagues report success or failure, they will have a lot to say about the chaos stage. Nobody looks forward to experiencing that uncomfortable stage.

ASSUMPTIONS ABOUT THE RIGHT WAY TO PROCEED. In the early 2000s, when hardly anyone had heard of Agile, few people approached its adoption with preconceived notions. Nowadays, a lot of people come to the table with assumptions, which they formed at their previous company, heard about from their software/IT colleagues, learned in a course, or read online — and their assumptions are all different! Some will just want to get started with anything, some will expect a checklist, some will insist on Scrum and others on Kanban, and so on.

You might experience additional complications not listed here. Some will apply to the entire team, while others will only apply to specific people. Overcoming them will take several conversations, one-on-one and with the entire team, over a few weeks. Consider enlisting the already-willing and excited to help you sway the neutral and objecting. Remember though: don't force Agile on people. Your goal is to get everyone ready, willing, and able to partake in an experiment that reflects some real change.

If the team hasn't read chapters 1 and 2 of this book yet, ask them to do so now. Point out what is *not* changing, and identify which elements of Agile they already happen to be using and how that's helping; doing that will reduce the perceived magnitude of the change. It might help to study chapter 7 together to gain a deeper shared understanding of the principles (otherwise, you'll do that as you start the experiment). Build trust and willingness to try a different way of working by being open, transparent, and realistic; it's okay to answer questions with "I don't know yet, but we'll find out together." Communicate in ways you know they'd appreciate, whether that's logic, or detailed explanations, or "go team!" speeches. Teach people the Satir Change Model, be forthright about the chaos period awaiting them, and promise your support. Be careful, though: do not portray the current way of working as old or wrong, as that's what people have been relying on to succeed by current standards.

When you chose the target of the first Agile experiment in chapter 4, you might have determined that the team needs to include members who are currently in separate functions or "silos." If you have any doubts that those folks would work well together — perhaps there's tension, mistrust, or history between them — removing those doubts should be your first priority. Sometimes it's as simple as creating opportunities for people to get to know and see each other as contributing workers who share and serve the same customers and organization. In tougher cases, you might need to have several sensitive private conversations to clear the air between people.

Five months ago, a director sought my help introducing Agile to his group. My brief assessment of the situation confirmed his hunch that implementing Agile in his group alone wouldn't be beneficial. For meaningful results, teams would need to include peers from another group, which was working in an agency model and presumably not open to collaboration with his staff. The director and his counterpart decided to build bridges between people before doing anything else about Agile. They put their entire staff, 20 people at a time, through my half-day collaboration workshop, where, in mixed groups, they experienced various forms of collaboration in a safe environment. Afterward, the directors created opportunities for cross-collaboration on real work. Slowly, they are seeing less "us vs. them" behaviors.

SUPPLEMENTARY RESOURCE: Download "Change Leadership: Preparation Questions" from the book's companion website, **AgileForNonSoftwareTeams.com**.

Prepare Yourself

Agile was born out of a disenchantment with heavy processes and hierarchical control of people's behaviors. Moving away from these elements requires empowering and supportive team-level leadership, psychological safety, and true collaboration. It calls for coaching instead of telling, advising, and rewarding. All this is on *you* to provide, although not on you alone. Many organizations continue to face challenges embracing Agile because they haven't built these capabilities. Their obvious leadership candidates — managers — possess little experience with these matters, having mostly worked in environments that were based on control, strict accountabilities, equating people with resources, and top-down decision-making.

For your group to become and *remain* Agile, your leadership style doesn't have to fit the Agile ideal, but it has to come close. Effective Agile change is inside out, bottom up, and top down — and you're in the center of it. You will have to truly put people first — ahead of deliverables, standards, and processes — if you want real Agility, not mere compliance with some checklist of Agile tactics. Your people will need you to trust them, to create a safe environment, to be consistent and reliable, to lead them toward a compelling vision, and to involve them in charting the course to the extent they're ready and able. They will need you to be sensitive to their experience with change and to support their often-challenging evolution as Agile practitioners.

None of this will be easy for you. Like them, you will also experience the Satir change curve, albeit at your own pace. Some of their decisions might worry you. You will encounter situations when you'll want to empower them, but feel that they're not ready for autonomy. You will have to deal with manifestations of the organizational culture that don't reward Agility, and with behaviors that keep established patterns in place. There will be times when you won't have a good answer, and the experts, books, or colleagues you'll consult will give you conflicting advice. Some "conventional wisdom" or expert Agile advice will not feel right.

The good news is that Agile adoption is not yours alone to succeed or fail at. It's a team effort, so err on the side of over-including your team. Given Agile's obsession with feedback, reflection, and improvement, you will be noticing problems a lot more than you used to. You won't solve all of them yourself; some will be the team's responsibility to solve, and some of those they may prefer not to deal with. As an Agile leader, you will experience a constant balancing act of guiding, empowering, offering solutions, and coaching. Just remember to *lead* more than you *manage.**

---

* Chapter 9 gives a few specific tips on leading vs. managing. For more, consult my book *The Human Side of Agile*.

Consider getting external help — someone to give you customized advice, training, and guidance — especially in the early stages. That person may be from elsewhere in your organization, or an independent expert; seek someone who is sensitive to your context and won't try to force-fit standard or software-specific methods.* If you're going for outside guidance but don't have the funds, consider waiting until you have them, because false starts are costly in both human and business terms.

Breanna Ramos, HR Associate, TechSmith:

"No matter how great the team is, sometimes trying to lead a change this large from inside — uprooting the way you work, trying to encourage new habits that don't feel comfortable in the beginning, trying to change fundamental beliefs about how our work functions — is difficult and nearly impossible to do cleanly. Getting an objective third party involved was the best decision we made."

John Hill, Agile Coach and Trainer:

"After some of our software development teams successfully switched to Kanban, the organization I'm coaching decided to have its service teams switch the same way. We brought the external Kanban trainer back in, and he trained the first service teams using the same material and exercises he'd used for the software teams. A senior leader in the service unit who attended this two-day class felt its focus on software made it irrelevant to anyone in the class and cancelled further sessions. This reaction opened our eyes to the fact that Agile software development practices sometimes have little value for service-oriented teams. We immediately pivoted, worked with the trainer to revamp the material and exercises to eliminate all references to developing software, and instead focused on service-oriented activities, which is now working."

---

* To see what I offer in this regard, head over to 3PVantage.com/services.

> **SUPPLEMENTARY RESOURCE**: Download "Considerations for Choosing Your Agile Coach" from the book's companion website, **AgileForNonSoftwareTeams.com**.

If you're bringing Agile to a group of 20 or more people, consider establishing a small Agile working group. This might be a virtual team if you need them to continue doing their day jobs. They will look after the care and feed of Agile by continuously strategizing about the journey and supporting their practitioner colleagues.

Lastly, remember: your Agile doesn't have to look like anyone else's. As long as you internalize the values and principles, how you make them a reality is your business and doesn't have to fit a mold or earn anyone's stamp of approval.

Even though each of the conversations, meetings, and reflections that make up these preparations might take only a couple of hours, they will likely span weeks or months. Don't rush them: they are important for maximizing the experiment's chance of success. When you're ready to start the experiment, invite everyone to read chapter 7 so they understand the principles better and what makes Agile agile, and follow chapter 8's guidance to design the initial workflow and team structure.

SUPPLEMENTARY RESOURCES

Go to **AgileForNonSoftwareTeams.com** and download "Change Leadership: Preparation Questions" and "Considerations for Choosing Your Agile Coach."

Chapter 7

Learn Enough About Agile Principles to Get Started

As explained in chapter 2, people's values and beliefs will guide their choice of operating principles. These, in turn, guide their choice and design of tactics, such as roles, process, practices, and artifacts. And while all organizations are different — even if they do similar work, they employ different people and have different cultures — those whose values and beliefs align with Agile tend to draw their principles from a consistent set. We saw a few of them in chapter 5: safety, respect, trust, and transparency. This chapter explains, as briefly and minimally as possible, a set of additional principles that you need to understand for chapter 8: designing your initial way of working. Chapters 9 and 10 will guide you in the first few months and beyond, expanding on those principles and introducing a few others.

Note: Earlier, you determined where to try Agile for the first time. If your analysis of values and beliefs yielded partial congruence with Agile, some of the following principles might feel irrelevant, inappropriate, or merely alien. Still, read and understand the full list so you can make informed design choices.

Organize People Around Value Creation

Most organizations are used to grouping people by function, role, or specialty. For instance, Person A is a designer who only does design work and is part of a design team. Person B, a risk analyst, is part of the risk team and only does risk-related work. In such organizations, the word "team" typically represents a group of people who do the same kind of work and report to the same functional manager. (That, by the way, is not the correct definition of the term "team.")

Many good intents justify this way of organizing people. By continuously applying their specialties, they become experts. Same-specialty colleagues working in proximity may help each other develop professionally and back each other up when necessary. With the guidance and support of their functional managers, they may establish the processes, adopt the tools, and optimize the practices that their specific work requires. The organization can treat them uniformly in terms of career growth and performance management.

Organizing functionally aligns well with a sequential or "hand-off" way of working. For instance: an account manager makes agreements with a customer, then an analyst compiles requirements, then a designer specifies a solution that satisfies the requirements, then other specialists build from the spec, then others test the deliverable for errors. The underlying assumption is that the specialist in each step can and should do a proper job so the specialists who follow can do theirs properly.

Like all choices, organizing people functionally has downsides. Usually, the worst offender is the specialists' tendency to focus on completing their *part*, losing sight of (or never knowing!) the product's or service's ultimate value and the context for its use. For example, if our creative team is putting together a brochure for the new product we'll promote at a trade show, it's not enough to have an attractive design and correct texts. Will our booth staff hand it to visitors during a conversation, or after it, or merely leave a stack of copies on the table? Will it compete with other information in the booth? Do we expect visitors to read the entire brochure? If not, which pieces should draw their limited attention? Should we even *have* a brochure, or something online? These questions don't doubt the team's professionalism; they have to do with *value* to our prospective customers and to our own organization. With specialists working in isolation, these questions may not be raised, or the answers may not be shared consistently among them; as a result, the deliverable may not be best fit for its purpose.

> I regularly write articles for professional magazines. After I submit an article, several editors modify my work without verifying anything with me, or even with each other. In a recent example, the word "Scrum" was consistently changed to "scrum." This little change in capitalization modifies the meaning of my writing, and is simply wrong. A reader who has even basic knowledge of Scrum would be justified in doubting the writer's knowledge.

The other contender to the "worst offender" title is the delay at each hand-off point. While the designer is working on her part, the content writer is not sitting idle; he is working on some other task. When the designer finishes, her design sits someplace, waiting for the content writer to free up. And when the writer discovers that some elements of the design have to change, the designer is busy with something else and can't get to them quickly. In many companies, delays of weeks and months due to hand-offs are *normal* (although a customer might find them incomprehensible or unacceptable). Because of that, project staff must start working very early, and the clients and stakeholders must articulate their needs much sooner than they are ready to do so. The work also costs more due to the increased need for "glue" — coordination and integration of separately produced pieces.

The lengthening of timelines causes another problem. When a specialist picks up a task, he or she has to figure out what to do, or what to change since the last time he or she worked on the artifacts. People are awful at remembering full details, so they ask colleagues, read notes, or make educated guesses. Colleagues might forget, remember incorrectly, or take time getting back with an answer. Written notes are usually incomplete, not quite accurate, or misunderstood. As a result, the assumption that every human link in the chain can do their work properly is often false. People do their best, but the quality and utility of the product degrades with every hand-off.

Agile's obsession with *customer delight* means avoiding organizing workers sequentially if at all possible. Instead of orienting individuals toward task completion, Agile orients teams toward value delivery — producing results that matter — and empowers the teams to decide how they'll produce that value. Every necessary person is part of the team, which makes the team "cross-functional." Team members are not clones and they might well have specialties, but their *responsibility*, and evidence of success, is that their collectively produced result accomplishes its intended outcome. While their contributions may not be equal, similar, or consistent throughout the work's life cycle, they don't disappear when they're less needed. If a team occasionally requires specialized work from departments that can't assign people on a full-time basis, it will form collaborative, quick-turnaround relationships with specific people in those departments.

A team that has fully dedicated members, always serves the same customers, and stays together over the long haul may realize outsized performance as a result of the strong relationships, knowledge, and mutual commitment the members build over time. This is a popular recommendation in Agile literature that focuses on software development or IT, where a product generally requires the same people to develop it over months or years. In your case, you might require a team to work toward diverse outcomes for different customers, sometimes in parallel. That doesn't compromise individual team members' potential for Agility, but it *does* require greater discipline around communication, decision-making, and task management.

To continue the trade show example, we would form a team to own our presence at the show (it might be disbanded soon thereafter, or remain in place for other shows). The team would include people knowledgeable about the particular product/service being promoted as well as a booth designer, a graphic designer, content writers, people who coordinate and negotiate with the event's organizers, and so on. Some of these specialists might be the same person. They would have close ties with important nonmembers in such departments as procurement, IT, and sales.

The team's customer is their company, and the outcome they pursue is increased market awareness of the product. How would they know which promotional activities would be valuable in that regard? If they have to make trade-offs, how would they compare options? If there's more work than they can handle, which parts should they forgo or work around? Ideally, the team's members have enough knowledge and autonomy to make the right calls on behalf of their company. Otherwise, they need someone, such as the product's manager or strategist, to make those calls.

Two IT executives at a top American university approached me for an assessment of their operations. Usually, getting to the starting line with a client — writing and signing a contract, registering my company as a vendor, issuing a purchase order, preparing documentation for cross-border travel — takes a couple of months, mostly made up of waiting. The two executives knew that if they waited this long, my assessment would not be very useful to them. So they teamed up with directors in Finance and Operations; all of us committed to turn artifacts around quickly; and they were able to relax some procedures, given the nature of the work and the risks involved. Within nine days, we were ready to go.

Collaborate on a Product, Service, or Solution

The business world has developed deep expertise in managing big work as *projects*. A project has a clear beginning and end, stakeholders, staff (sometimes dehumanized as "resources"), timelines, and budgets. It also has deliverables, which can be of many kinds. For instance, a project may yield artifacts, such as a risk model; it may replace an existing thing, such as an old system with a modern system; it may produce a new business process, for example when replacing manual data-entry with an automated process.

Some work is "one and done": the team makes the deliverable in one shot, gives it to the customer, and can theoretically forget all about it. For any other work, Agile favors treating the object of that work as a *product* — a higher standard than generic *deliverables* — reflecting the following characteristics:

- ✦ Products have a life cycle, extending both before and after their making: they are envisioned, made, maintained, improved, modified, and eventually retired.

✦ Products have customers and users, whether internal or external, whom they help to achieve outcomes: solve problems (pain points), address needs, and accomplish goals.

✦ The relationship that customers and users have with their products has an emotional dimension. They need to *want* those specific products and to know how to use them, otherwise they'll get their needs met some other way. Customers often require some kind of support both getting started ("change management") and through continued usage ("customer service").

✦ Focusing workers on making products, rather than completing a set of tasks, seems to keep the workers motivated and to yield results that matter more to the customers.

Think of products you own that enhance your personal life on some dimension, and how they are more than the sum of their parts and functions: car, phone, sunglasses, exercise equipment, online subscriptions, and so on. Similarly, you also benefit from services that are more than the performance of tasks: meal delivery, club memberships, dry cleaning, and the like. Thinking in terms of "product" or "service" (or "solution") captures the richness of doing something that makes a difference to someone who wants it.

For an example of a business-oriented product, consider your company's website. It is much more than a collection of Web technologies, texts, and graphics. Its content, flow, "contact us" page, special offers, landing pages, keywords, "subscribe to our newsletter," and myriad other components must work together to invite the visiting user to engage with the company. It's a product, even if it had been originally produced as a deliverable from a project. It will be in use for years, undergoing both regular maintenance and occasional overhauls, and at some point it will be retired.

For an example of a service, take the employee on-boarding process. In many companies, it is a set of tasks for various people: prepare a desk, create system access credentials, conduct a welcome conversation, fill in HR forms, and on and on. Other companies,[1] on the other hand, see the smooth, feel-good integration of a new person as a service with three customers: the new person, the team they join, and the entire organization. The life cycle of this service would include follow-ups and adjustments (not only by the hiring manager), as well as drawing lessons from the experience of on-boarding one employee to improve the process for the next one. The "service" approach seems to take more effort, but likely increases retention and performance.

Another common downside of project thinking is the divide between the doers and their beneficiaries. When they work in different businesses or in an agency model, this divide seems inevitable. For example, when I interviewed designers for my first book and its website, all of them expected a hand-off and a fixed-price contract, neither of which invites a positive, synergistic relationship. Inside an organization, it's a similar dynamic when people work in different functions or units; for instance, when IT selects, procures, installs, and configures an accounting software system, they are likely to see their customers (people in Accounting) mostly at the beginning and end of the process. In too many projects, the relationship between the team and their customers is that of order-taking, and if the customers are regularly involved in the process, that is in a bossy, micromanaging, or mistrustful manner.

> Liz S., Marketing Manager at a technology company:
>
> "The Marketing Operations leader was our product owner. He was the sole decision-maker, and we had zero visibility into his priorities. This stifled our creativity, and we lost connection with the marketing analysts. There was a ton of back and forth between the creative world and operational world, but we weren't talking to each other; it was all 'Please update the ticket.' We felt like robots."

The Agile mind-set is quite emphatic about *not* having this kind of relationship if at all possible. To wit, one of the four values is "customer collaboration." The customers are still that — beneficiaries of the work, users of its results, sometimes paying for it — but they act as *partners*. It's a two-way street between the customers, who seek outcomes of value, and the empowered teams who figure out how to accomplish those outcomes. Some companies have adopted the term "business partner" instead of "product owner," to emphasize the point.

> Words that often get conflated in this discussion are *customer* (or client), *stakeholder*, and *user* (or consumer). In many situations, they are different people or groups and have different outcomes, but Agile encourages the doers to have a collaborative, caring relationship with all of them. For instance, a life insurance company would naturally want to have a good relationship with its paying policyholders, but it should have an even more empathetic relationship with the beneficiaries of deceased policyholders, who don't pay the company anything.[2] For simplicity, I refer to them in this book by the single word *customer*.

Customer collaboration takes many forms. There are frequent conversations (ideally, but not necessarily, face to face) to elicit real needs and weigh options. Team members frequently demonstrate interim accomplishments for early feedback and adjustment. The team feels safe to raise suggestions, articulate risks, even say that they're behind. Both sides make the effort to build a relationship that should produce great results *and* have them working together again for additional successes.

Produce Outcomes of Value

When people talk about their work, they will often describe inputs (activities, tasks) and the outputs they produce (deliverables). For example, to achieve the deliverable called "streamlined hiring process," HR's activities might include a gap analysis, a study of current literature for options, and updating templates and procedures. Or, to add an Agile leadership course to an organization's internal training roster, Learning & Development might issue a request for proposals, interview potential trainers, run a trial session, and so on.

Talking about the work in terms of inputs and outputs is *easy*. It's tangible and familiar. It's what people put on plans, keep track of, and hold others accountable for. The Agile mind-set — particularly its values of "people first" and "customer collaboration" — reminds everyone to take a step back from inputs and outputs and ask about their *outcomes*: "What's the purpose of this task?" "How will the deliverable matter?" "What will happen as a result?"

Consider the HR and Learning examples. Which outcomes would an organization expect a streamlined hiring process to accomplish: Higher productivity, fewer bad hires, greater staff diversity, or something else? Which outcomes should Agile leadership training produce: Better culture, higher team engagement, smoother delivery? When you have multiple answers, it's helpful to focus on the one or two that most justify doing the work, and then use them to guide further choices. Better yet, start by identifying the outcomes that matter, and then figure out the deliverables that will achieve them!

Put another way, outcomes are the problems, needs, or goals you're after. The deliverables are the ways you'll solve those problems, fulfill those needs, or accomplish those goals.

Correctly identifying the outcomes increases alignment among the participants: they are all doing this work for the same reasons. When having to make decisions along the way, knowing the outcome helps them make good decisions. Comparing work items based on their intended outcomes helps them determine which ones to finish earlier. Outcomes motivate people and keep them engaged if the work takes a while. They invite creativity and suppress the "here is how we always work on this type of thing" tendency.

One Finance department produces a monthly report showing each managing director's discretionary spending vs. budget. The report is an internal standard procedure, not mandated by any compliance requirement. I asked the head of Finance, "What are a typical director's outcomes for the report?" After some reflection, we narrowed down the list: each managing director wants to know how much they have for staff development/conferences/travel/recognition; to be reminded of their accumulated spend and whether they're heading into trouble; and to know what they should worry about (including deadlines). Finance cares about two additional outcomes: keeping their spending projection current and avoiding gross overspending. Having listed out everyone's outcomes, the head of Finance realized that her team can accomplish them with simpler, quicker reporting supplemented by an in-person meeting every other month.

When you are mindful of outcomes rather than focused only on outputs, you have a chance of *doing less work*. Instead of slogging through the initially envisioned scope of work, the team might stop sooner because they can tell they have enough. Or, they might reconsider their suggested solution and find one that takes less work. Back to the Learning & Development example: once you know the problem, need, or goal for which Agile leadership training is a possible solution, would a book club or buddy-coaching be a better solution?

An Agile team generally pursues the following five, partially overlapping categories of outcomes:

A. Address a problem, need, or goal of the customer.

B. Mitigate an important risk (e.g., technical viability, consumer appeal, legal hurdle).

C. Learn, or obtain meaningful feedback, about something important (e.g., "Do we know and understand the potential side effects of delivering X?" "Will people use deliverable Y enough to justify making it?").

D. Make it possible for their business to seize a specific opportunity (e.g., have something to demo or promote at an upcoming trade conference).

E. Enable or facilitate delivering value later (e.g., consolidate client data into a single system; book location and speakers for a company off site).

Agile teams compare and sequence outcomes on the basis of their *value*. Outcome A is about value to the *customer*: making the customer more successful.[3] Outcomes B through E provide *business* value: they address problems, needs, and goals of the entity doing the work; they make the business more likely to succeed. Each outcome may be accomplished through a series of mini-outcomes, each of which also falls into the above categories. Most of a team's effort ought to produce A outcomes (customer value); of those, the team would work first on mini-outcomes that provide the highest value and/or incur the highest cost if they're delayed.

Always Work on What's Most Important

As much as possible, Agile teams try to finish work on one outcome at a time, rather than spread themselves thin trying to achieve multiple ones (which delays all of them). If along the way they encounter *impediments* to finishing — anything that makes it hard, slow, or awkward to finish work — they try to remove or mitigate them. While working on one outcome, they might think or hear about the next one, but prefer not to start working on it. This obsession with finishing as soon as possible is colloquially known as "getting to 'done'."

Whatever a deliverable happens to be, the work to produce it boils down to a sequence of tasks or "work items": activities that yield some outputs that contribute to the eventual deliverable. Some tasks are conceptual while others are tangible; some tasks create artifacts while others check them; some tasks might have to be done sequentially, while others might be done in parallel by different people. What do these tasks focus on, and how is that determined?

Suppose your work is to build a new house on an empty lot. Once you have the blueprints, the sequence of construction tasks would probably look like this: excavate, pour the foundation, put up the walls, lay the floors, put up the roof, and so on. The principle behind this set of tasks is to have a single efficient pass. The sequence *makes sense* for several reasons. Constructing houses is a solved problem: there are well-established methods that produce predictable results. Some activities must follow others, and performing each step correctly minimizes the cost of later steps. Neither the customer nor the builder should change the house significantly during or after construction, because that's expensive, and they *can* make their big decisions up front.

In chapter 2, I referred to such reasons as beliefs: assumptions big enough that they influence how you choose to work. An Agile approach shines when you hold a different set of beliefs: you might not get everything right the first time, you might improve your methods as you work, and you might have legitimate reasons to change direction mid-work (or after the product is considered finished).

If you choose to work this way — if you "optimize for" adaptation — then a single efficient pass may not be the best principle for determining and sequencing the tasks. A more appropriate choice would be to keep asking "What's the most important thing to do now?" Every answer would involve adding a piece or changing an existing piece; that is why Agile work is known as *iterative and incremental*, or *evolutionary*.

For example, take the writing of this book. After reviewing my outline with potential readers, I wrote the text one section at a time. However, during that time, I often realized that I needed to make changes elsewhere: convey concepts differently, rearrange sections or chapters, remove duplication, or replace examples. I usually finished the section I was working on before making those changes. Within each section, I worked the same way on a smaller scale — that of the paragraph. After finishing the first draft, I reread it and my research notes, and found dozens of points and changes to make. My process was highly exploratory and adaptive. Contrast it with the single-pass alternative, wherein I'd start with a very detailed outline, expand every point into a section, then review or ask for feedback about a presumably completed book. That process would be costly if the feedback showed I'd gotten some of the fundamentals wrong.

In an iterative and incremental process, mid-work *change* is welcome if the potential increase in the product's ultimate value is worth the cost of iteration.* The people doing the work might be proactive about changes by coming up with their own ideas (as in my writing example) or by soliciting others' feedback. They can also be reactive, receiving suggestions and requests from others with a stake in the work. Agile's value of "customer collaboration" guides the team to regularly seek (and prefer) the feedback of the work's beneficiaries, or the closest proxies they have access to, rather than that of their managers. There's a balance to strike: on one hand, don't work too long without feedback; on the other, don't ask for it too often to nag people, receive input that's too small to matter, or create a drag on progress.

When using a single-pass process, as in the house-building example, determining tasks is largely a matter of sequencing mini-deliverables

---

* The extreme and wasteful form of iteration is rework: throwing the result out and starting over. Rework rarely occurs when a team follows the other principles mentioned in this chapter.

by dependencies. Now, let's consider another example: a department's management has identified the need for a new leadership role. The deliverables for this outcome include: job description, title, compensation structure, hiring process, and job posting. A single-pass process might be as simple as producing each of these five mini-deliverables in the given order, relying on familiar artifacts or industry standards. It "makes sense": get the job description right, so you can get the title right, and then the compensation structure right, and so forth.

However, if the role is nonstandard and getting it right is critical *(are you beginning to recognize such phrases as values and beliefs?)*, it would make sense to design it adaptively. When using an iterative and incremental process, the task sequence front-loads decisions that would be costly to change, and makes room for frequent feedback. It is also likely that some mini-deliverables evolve across tasks. In this example, the following sequence could work well (the italicized text explains the tasks' reasons or possible effects):

1. Sketch out the purpose of the role.

2. Draft the role's level, authority, reporting line, and accountabilities. *These might trigger a change to the purpose.*

3. Consider potential gains and risks arising from having this role, such as to departmental culture, team effectiveness, or individual motivation. *These insights might enhance or change the work done in #1 and #2. They might even have you reconsider the rationale for the new role.*

4. Determine the characteristics of a successful candidate. *If they imply that the company already has enough internal candidates, that might affect the above choices.*

5. Determine compensation structure or salary range. *This might cause a reality check.*

The next tasks could be: create job description, determine hiring process, produce job posting. Since you've iterated on the big-ticket items, any changes triggered by these tasks should have a low cost.

Working in this iterative and incremental manner helps you *do more of the right and less of the wrong*. A useful practice in this regard is to evolve outcomes through three evolutionary milestones called "Earliest Testable/ Usable/Lovable."[4] The Earliest Testable thing (product, service, solution) enables you to test your hypotheses about the outcome and suitable deliverables; it provides *learning*. The Earliest Usable thing accomplishes the customer's outcome minimally; it delivers basic *value*. The Earliest Lovable expands on the outcome and its value; it delivers *delight*.

I use this progression when preparing new conference sessions, such as presentations or workshops. My Earliest Testable session is not an actual presentation but the proposal to the program committee: the session's title and description, learning objectives and key messages, and a rough idea of the delivery format for each. If the organizers accept my proposal, I know that we agree on the session's value, that I've mitigated some design risks, and that I should develop the actual session. (If they reject my proposal, my overall investment has been small.) My Earliest Usable session delivers minimally on its learning objectives: I have the session design, my main points are in a mostly textual slide deck, and I've practiced it enough to know that it fits in the allotted time. The Earliest Lovable session increases the value to the audience; to get there, I replace texts with appropriate visuals, firm up the opening and closing, and fine-tune my timing, stories, and turns of phrase. For an additional example of the Testable/Usable/Lovable progression, read endnote 5 for chapter 7.

If you've interpreted this principle of "always work on what's most important" as "one thing at a time," you wouldn't be wrong. Theoretically, you *can* work on one outcome without knowing anything about later ones. Realistically, though, you have to give special consideration to date-constrained future work and to dependencies. It also makes sense to think ahead, so you can make informed promises and commitments (if needed) and identify some opportunities for removing waste. How far ahead depends on your context. You might have to identify a sequence of outcomes already at the beginning of the work, especially if you need to align multiple people around it. Most Agile teams capture their future work in a *product backlog*: a single, always-prioritized master list of valuable deliverables they might get to. They make small incremental commitments based on what's currently at the top of that backlog and what they must start because of dependencies and date expectations. Unfortunately, many teams treat their *entire* backlog as a commitment rather than as options — basically, they use it as a project plan — and thus severely limit their ability to be adaptive.

Get Feedback Frequently

Outcomes might be your North Star, but on a day-to-day basis, it's activities and deliverables that command your attention. How do you know that your deliverables would, in fact, yield the intended outcomes? Put another way, how do you know you're working *effectively*?

Most people in most organizations don't ask this question. Instead, they obsess over efficiency, which is all about minimizing waste during the work. Waste — of time, money, effort, goodwill — occurs when people do redundant work, relearn forgotten procedures, wait for others, fix defects, and otherwise do things that don't add value.

Nobody wants to incur waste or sets out to make it, yet it's everywhere, in spades. Should you focus your efforts on detecting, analyzing, and eliminating process waste in order to increase efficiency? The answer is "yes" if you make a fundamental assumption that is *not* an Agile one: that you're producing the right thing. For instance, if you have a factory that turns out thousands of copies of the same physical product, definitely try to remove waste from your production process.

However, what if you make fundamentally different assumptions? What if you believe that you could be wrong? That you don't, can't, or shouldn't try to have all the answers up front? That there might be big surprises once you deliver what you think now is right? Those are Agile beliefs, and they give rise to a specific Agile principle: first be effective, then be efficient. Other ways of saying this are "get bad news early," "fail fast," and "learn fast." Great! Now, *how?*

The traditional strategy for maximizing effectiveness and efficiency is planning. Think long and hard, engage experts, ask all the right questions, and once you're certain, put a plan together for efficient execution. As the saying goes, "Measure twice, cut once." If this approach sounds right for your needs — not merely familiar — go for it. If it's not, the Agile answer is to seek and apply feedback *during* the work. Design your methods to facilitate getting practical feedback on risky/assumed work. Use the feedback both to validate what you do and to consider needed adaptation, in case your initial intents are not a guaranteed success. Be aware, though, that this is much harder than it seems for a variety of reasons:

- ✦ The feedback must come from relevant sources.

- ✦ You have to receive it in a timely fashion.

- ✦ The feedback providers must feel safe, and pay enough attention, to give you useful feedback, including negative comments.

- ✦ You have to be open and confident enough to process it.

- ✦ There needs to be a clear process for deciding what to do with the feedback, especially if multiple sources offer contradictory opinions.

Chris Armstrong, Design Director at Operative Brand Consulting:

"When starting to work on brand identity projects, we brainstorm a large number of ideas internally, and arrive at three different concepts that we present to the client. Each concept is a distinct approach that fulfills our strategic criteria. Even though this is arguably less efficient than preparing a single concept, clients need to have options due to the subjective nature of visual design work. Following client feedback, we will create a single refined direction, often combining elements from the different concepts. Some clients might ask us up front to show a larger number of different concepts; we explain to them that a greater quantity doesn't usually translate to improved quality and doesn't justify the cost of working up extra concepts."

In addition to the emotional challenges of giving and receiving feedback, the whole process around it requires a substantial amount of time from the team. The Agile assumption is that the likelihood of being wrong, and thereby not delighting the customer or having to rework a lot, is high enough to justify spending this time. As you start thinking of designing your own Agile process, you'll have to consider whether you agree with this, and how much you're willing to spend on (or wait for) feedback. An hour-long demo meeting every two weeks — a popular practice among software development teams — might be just right, or not. You might need different feedback processes for different types of work. The key is to be effective first and efficient second.

Russ Dickerson, Hardware Engineering Director, Synapse Wireless:

"We were used to delivering finished designs to Production. Now, we regularly give them early designs and they do a mock build for us. This gives us useful feedback early on, facilitates integration later on, and creates collaboration between our groups."

SUPPLEMENTARY RESOURCE: Download "Gil Broza's Process for Effective Feedback Requests" from the book's companion website, **AgileForNonSoftwareTeams.com**.

Keep the Cost of Change Low

If you're always thinking about outcomes, collaborating with your customer, and prizing effectiveness, you're probably frequently deciding what to do next and how to do it. In that, Agile represents a major shift from traditional project planning where these decisions are made early, big-bang style. Agile planning does retain similarities to traditional planning in weighing options also by the cost of the work and the team's capacity.

There is one more consideration, called the *cost of change*: you have to think ahead, understand which of today's choices could bite you later, and work accordingly. In my experience, most Agile practitioners don't pay enough attention to the cost of change, sometimes compromising their otherwise good attention to value, effectiveness, and feedback. Don't let this happen to you!

A certain technology company regularly hosts large trade events, which require extensive printing (handouts, signage, etc.). It is not uncommon for an executive to come in a few days before show time and object to some of those texts, despite earlier approvals. These last-minute changes — getting the new texts right, and reprinting and redistributing all the affected material — are costly and stressful.

Both while working on a deliverable *and* after it's presumably "done," you face five broad categories of justifiable change. You may decide to, or have to:

+ Pursue a different outcome (problem/need/goal)

+ Produce a different deliverable/solution to accomplish a given outcome

+ Add/change features, elements, or aspects of the deliverable

+ Make the deliverable more efficient, robust, or general

+ Correct mistakes or choices made in the preparation of the deliverable

When such changes are expensive, traditional planning approaches (such as classical project management) try to *prevent* them. These approaches front-load the work with all the hard thinking about all the big questions, intending to limit the need to change. This is a valid principle if people can figure out those matters up front. For instance, a movie's producers will select the actors long before filming starts, and avoid replacing them during production. Another popular principle is to set aside time for the workers to react to changes, such as by padding the estimates or by "freezing" artifacts far enough ahead of the anticipated finish date. A third principle is to postpone some of the work to a point in time when no more changes will occur; for instance, a Technical Publications team might document a product's features only once the product is fully developed.

Agile is adaptive and responsive. It welcomes change and prepares for it using short work cycles, customer involvement, flexible backlogs, and collaboration. A common mistake practitioners make is seeing change as free, or not trying to understand its cost. The team has made something, and now there's a better idea? Put it on the backlog of work to be done later. If it's important enough, it will get done instead of lower-importance things. That's it.

However, the cost of a later change is usually *not* the straight cost of the work, because there's already an existing solution to reckon with. Think of HR forms, marketing material, customer data systems, and the office layout; whatever it cost to make them the first time, changing anything later — voluntarily or otherwise — may cost a lot more because you're not starting from scratch.[6]

Cost-of-change thinking applies already in the design of the way of working. For instance, when I started writing my first book, *The Human Side of Agile*, I had only a vague idea of what it would say, and intended to iterate and seek feedback on the content frequently; the content thus had the highest cost of change in terms of my time and effort. Therefore, I chose to make the manuscript easy to share, review, and edit by writing it in a single large Word document; only when the content was final did I port it to the various publishing formats. When writing my second book, *The Agile Mind-Set*, I had most of the content already in my head and didn't expect many changes. Therefore, I wrote on Leanpub, a platform that makes frequent publishing easy but reviewing and commenting quite cumbersome; it allowed me to get the e-book format out early. Consider these two projects: same kind of work, same author, same goals and values, but a different process as a consequence of cost-of-change thinking.

Some custom software development companies use "co-teaming" as a strategy for containing the cost of change and increasing effectiveness. Instead of working in their own office and communicating with client staff electronically and infrequently, the vendor's team relocates temporarily to the client's office and works in the same space as their direct client contacts. That allows them to establish ways of working that rely on frequent face-to-face interactions. By reducing delays and increasing collaboration and trust, they reduce the likelihood of costly late changes.

You can't eliminate the cost of change, but do what you can to minimize it. At planning junctures, look at work items — including small and innocuous ones — through the lens of "What headache could changing these later cause us?" (whether such changes are voluntary or imposed!). Additional examples of process choices that implement this principle include:

+ Remove duplication. The more copies or derivatives you keep of something, the more places you'll have to change (and likely all at the same time!).

+ Simplify. Dial back on elements and avoid components that increase value only marginally. For instance, I design course handouts and materials for black-and-white printing; color would add little value to my students, while requiring more effort to keep consistent.

+ Allow "undo." Any work you do on a computer, use software that can reverse steps you took. For instance, some word processing apps save versions as you work and allow you to revert to a previous version.

Constrain the Intake of Work

Imagine you have to drive someplace for a meeting. You take the ramp onto the highway, merge with a bit of difficulty, and within 30 seconds the traffic slows down to a crawl. You spend 20 minutes more on the highway than you would had you taken another route.

Imagine instead that before you get to the ramp, an electronic sign advises you that the highway is congested. Or that an app on your phone does that. Or that before you leave, you learn that traffic is bad everywhere, and manage to reschedule the meeting or even conduct it online from your current location.

As drivers and commuters, we use the options in the second scenario more and more. Yet, at work, people tend to be stuck in the first scenario. Think of your team as the highway, moving people in vehicles (work items) to their destination (completion/delivery). If the team is busy, what's the likelihood they'll add even more tasks to their list, and get bogged down even more?

Given labor costs, managers naturally want to keep people busy. Workers, for their part, want to be productive. Some take pride or pleasure in being busy, having "a lot on their plate," and finding creative ways to cram more work into their schedules. All of that work may well be important, just as every driver on the highway is there for a reason. The problem here is not with busyness; it is with *finishing* – getting to one's destination. When workers process too many items, they delay finishing most of them, compromise the quality of their work, struggle to meet commitments, and run themselves ragged.[7]

In the desired alternative, called "flow," workers focus their attention on finishing some items early, then finishing another few items, and so on. Flow respects the beliefs that finishing matters more than starting, and that starting more work than can be finished is false productivity. Flow allows teams to act on their commitments and to be reliable and trusted partners.

To achieve flow, teams must constrain their work intake. Discovering their capacity for moving work all the way from start to finish, they impose artificial constraints on themselves to avoid taking on more work than they can realistically complete. Two popular constraints, which may be combined but don't have to be, are:

1. Plan and execute in small time-boxes. A team determines a short duration and plans by asking, "What's the best thing we can do in this time-box?" When the time runs out, they plan what to do in the next time-box. This is the default mode in Agile, where these time-boxes are called "iterations" or "sprints" and often last no longer than a week or two.

2. Limit work-in-progress (WIP). A team determines a low number, such as five, three, or one, and never works on more items than that at a given time. When they find themselves with fewer items in flight, they may take more, up to the limit, though they'd do better to finish the ones in flight. This prin-

ciple is fundamental to the Kanban method, and Agile teams find it useful as well.

In both cases, the constraint must be tight enough to force people to seriously prioritize their work and make tradeoffs. If the time-box is several weeks long,* or the WIP limit too high, the constraint is meaningless and the team is back to taking on a lot of work.

Regardless of how teams capture and maintain the body of anticipated work, they must have an easy way of determining which of the items they'll *pull* into their time-box or work queue. To minimize planning delays, teams might also spend some of their time thinking through those next items ("refining" or "grooming" them) a few days before committing to them. There is a balance to strike there. When the list of next items is short, planning is more responsive and "just in time," but the team runs a higher risk of "starving" when they're ready for more work. When the list is long, the team is being more predictive and likely less adaptive. The key is that at any given point, nobody is delaying important work from finishing, either by processing more items than they can realistically finish or by preparing for potentially unneeded work.

Notice my vague reference above to "the body of anticipated work." Chances are your team processes work items from multiple sources, such as project tasks, one-off requests, and recurring obligations. These work items also arrive on multiple channels: task management applications, email, calendar reminders, and in-person conversations. To ensure effective prioritization and capacity-based planning, it is critical to funnel everything into as few channels as possible so it's easy to track items and compare their value and cost of delay. As mentioned earlier, many Agile teams opt for a single such channel — the backlog — which they keep constantly updated. What they "refine" or "groom" is the top of that backlog.

---

* Older literature on Agile recommended iteration/sprint length of up to 30 days. These days, blocking off and planning for this much undisturbed time, without intermediate feedback and adaptation points, doesn't seem practical for most kinds of work. Hence, most teams use cycles of one or two weeks.

Visualize the Work

Deliverables from work are usually visible or tangible. As people produce them, they might prepare interim or temporary artifacts — a sketch on a whiteboard, a list of ideas on paper, a model. Agile teams also make their *work items* visible. More specifically, they *visualize* the content and state of those items. They don't settle for lowly to-do lists or merely writing tasks down; they want to *see* everything they deal with in a form that makes supporting *flow* and *manipulating* any item easy.

The most common manifestation of this principle is *the board*: a physical or electronic board indicating everything the team is actively working on or is about to begin. Boards have columns that correspond to the team's workflow. A column on the left, typically called "Ready," lists all the items that are ready for the team to work on next (if the team uses sprints/iterations, it will show all the items intended for the time-box of the sprint). The items that are in flight appear in the next columns based on the state they're in. The rightmost column, "Done," lists everything that the team recently committed to and has recently finished. The rest of the backlog is kept separately and within easy reach, because what a team wants to know about current items is different than what it cares about for later items.

Teams design their boards, and the cards that represent work items, to communicate useful information. For example, they might divide the board into "swim lanes" — horizontal bands — to call out different classes of items such as project work, recurring work ("business as usual"), and emergencies. They might color-code cards to communicate some important message, such as criticality or constraint. They will have made a team agreement about the kind of text that goes on each card, and if it's not the full description of the work item, where and how to capture the rest of it.

An early-days example from a marketing team. The leftmost column, "Brainstorm," contains sticky notes representing items they're considering but haven't committed to. The next column, "Plan," has all the items they've committed to but haven't started yet. Items go through several activities; after finishing an activity for a given work item, the team will move it to below the horizontal line, signaling it's ready to be pulled into the next stage. Eventually, items get to "In Market" and, some time later, their effect gets measured. Colors indicate different business activities, such as brand marketing and product marketing. The size of a sticky note corresponds to the size of its work item.

On the most basic level, a board (whether physical or electronic) has several benefits:

+ It's easy to detect omissions and planning errors, because everything is in one place.

+ When adding or reprioritizing a work item, it's easy to see what other work it would delay, or whether other work trumps it.

+ A board creates a focal point for the team's attention and promotes transparency. If it's a physical board, it becomes a place for the team to congregate.

+ Everyone can see what's in flight (middle columns) and what's coming up (left columns), which increases their sense of control over their work — a critical component of job satisfaction.

Visualizing the state of work items is particularly helpful for seeing flow, or, more usefully, seeing when it's hampered. By observing the movement of individual items, teams can detect systemic patterns, such as bottlenecks and imbalances, that hinder their ability to deliver value.

A team owns their board's design *and* operation. For instance, when members start or finish some work on an item, they move its sticky note on the board to communicate the state change. This seemingly trivial act reinforces *team-level* ownership, responsibility, and self-organization. And as an added benefit, anyone interested in project status can now self-serve simply by looking at the board, without having to interrupt or nag people for updates.

The design of a team board will reinforce principles and behaviors whether they are desirable or not. For example, it is generally helpful to indicate who is (or are!) working on each item. Doing that by assigning swim lanes to specific team members reinforces solo work and invites maximization of individual workload. By contrast, assigning swim lanes to kinds of work and indicating who's doing what by using a removable avatar, such as a picture on a magnet, focuses attention on the work and thus reinforces collaboration and shared ownership.

Break Work Down

You're probably already used to managing large work and small work differently. You don't put "Get a university degree" on your weekly plan, and you don't put "Renovate the kitchen" on a daily plan or to-do list. Instead, when you face large deliverables, you *decompose* (split) them into smaller actions and mini-deliverables that build up to the larger ones. With an Agile mind-set, you'll have a particular discipline regarding work items: making them *small* and *meaningful*.

- ✦ A work item is meaningful if it yields a mini-outcome as explained in "Produce Outcomes of Value": it addresses a portion of a problem/need/goal of the customer, allows for learning and feedback, reduces some risk, seizes a timely opportunity, or enables later value delivery.* Notice how different such items might be from activity-focused tasks that might be assigned to specialists.

✦ A work item is small if it's easy for the team to see the end of it, whether due to the required effort (say, a couple of days or less) or to the level of complexity and unknowns.

Breaking work down this way is key to Agility. You're always close to finishing a small item. When it's done, switching to some other task, pausing, or rethinking your course of action is easy. Since it's small, you can understand and control its impact, including its effect on future costs of change. Since the item is meaningful, you're in a position to deliver value (even though it's partial) or at least to seek feedback early. And across several such items, it will be easy to see progress, as well as bottlenecks and delays.

Taking on larger work items, on the other hand, limits Agility. If they take multiple days or weeks on average, constraining their intake or visualizing them won't be useful. As a work item sits in an "in progress" state, you won't truly know what's going on with it: How much work remains? Which parts are stalled? What kind of collaboration could help it along? You'll also be more likely to soldier on with the work and miss opportunities to cut your losses.

When you decompose large work the Agile way, you may not need to create a complete work breakdown structure. You can keep some of the later work underspecified until you need to decompose it. This is an application of the Lean principle called "defer decisions to the last responsible moment."

---

* "User stories" are a popular (but not the only) way to capture what I refer to here as meaningful work items. A story generally contains at least three key pieces of information: *what* the deliverable/solution is, *who* will use it, and *why* it's valuable (what outcome it serves).

Consider this example: a business wants to do content marketing using a series of seven short videos, which educate viewers on various topics and invite them to click through to the company's services page. The high-level task sequence might start with:

1. Identify viewer persona and journey in the context of the company's overall marketing approach.

2. Choose and sequence the seven topics. *Ask a few potential viewers for feedback.*

3. Write the newsletter and social media posts that will launch the series (don't post them yet). *This will provide input to the videos' content.*

4. Script the first video; get feedback on both the script and the promotional content from multiple sources, looking particularly for red flags.

5. Script the other videos.

6. Shoot all the videos.

If task #1 is large, it may be broken down to research, drafts, and refinement. Splitting task #3, its first two subtasks might be:

1. Draft the newsletter, using placeholders for images. *Drafting promotional text first will help us learn how to describe the videos and what the viewers will get from them.*

2. Come up with two short messages and create them in different formats for the targeted social media channels.

Once the team is done with tasks #1-4, they'll get more specific about later items. For instance, the first task in #6 might be "Use a smartphone to shoot a dry run of video #1, and run the unedited video by some people."

Bounded Team Autonomy

Earlier, we looked at choosing and sequencing tasks. What we *didn't* look at was who does the choosing and sequencing, or any decision-making around task execution. Once again, values and beliefs inform the answers.

Traditional ways of working value control and predictability. In control, the more authorized tell the less authorized what to do when. In predictability, workers and managers are supposed to follow policies and standard operating procedures and to minimize independent judgment. That's good for some purposes, but agility isn't one of them.

In an Agile way of working, the choice of outcomes to pursue, and sometimes the choice of deliverables to produce, are often made by people closest to the customer and/or by senior managers (because the choices have ramifications beyond the team). However, much of the tactical decision-making lies in the hands of those closest to the work. That means the individual workers and their teams can make many binding decisions instead of a supervisor, manager, project manager, stakeholder, or even their own team lead (or, they don't need their approval). They are trusted to act with a high degree of autonomy, but it is bounded. The boundaries include organizational culture, policies, guardrails, strategic choices, and other system constraints. The degree of freedom is high, but cowboy behaviors are not welcome.

One reason (belief, really) underlying this choice is that the workers are generally more knowledgeable about the work's details than those approving their decisions. Another reason is the delay inherent to seeking and receiving approvals. A third reason is that the reality on the ground is usually more nuanced than a set of policies can ever cover, and thus calls for decision-making by the most informed. The most powerful reason, which is often invisible, is that some level of autonomy is needed for keeping people both engaged and motivated. People who have little control over their work will put in only the minimum effort to check a box.

In Agile, the unit that produces deliverables to achieve outcomes is the cross-functional team. Thus, it's the team that has bounded autonomy; individual members have it to the extent that it supports the team's goals and well-being. The boundaries are typically drawn on a case-by-case basis.

To continue the trade show booth example given in "Organize People Around Value Creation" on page 75, the booth designer cannot unilaterally decide to radically change the booth's design. The entire team would need to reach consensus on design changes, since they might affect the outcomes and the needed work. As a *team*, they are empowered to make any booth-related decisions that do not materially affect the company's trade show presence or its other commitments.

Self-Organization

The team's autonomy includes the ability to self-organize: to decide who does what when. Having determined the next few tasks, team members determine who will do the first ones; later, when someone frees up, he or she chooses the next one from that small set. In doing so, they consult each other and perhaps even people outside the team, but it's ultimately their call. As much as possible, they make their decisions with *consensus*: having heard everyone's voice, everyone commits to act on those decisions (whether they loved them or not) so that the team may move forward.

As mentioned earlier, finishing matters more than starting: Agile teams prefer to move "in progress" items to "done" over moving "ready" items to "in progress." Naively, that can be accomplished by each member taking on one task at a time, and doing it from start to finish. A team may achieve better flow — a more even rate of finishing — by shifting tasks among members, collaborating, or cooperating. Often, such actions will be more successful when triggered by self-organization (that is, by the team members themselves) than when mandated, controlled, or orchestrated by others.

In most environments, the majority of the staff are specialists: they are particularly skilled or knowledgeable in a small set of areas needed for the work. A minority are generalists: they are reasonably competent in many areas of the work. While a team may possess all the necessary skills represented, their distribution among the members might not be efficient for the work. For example, if a team has only one member who can perform risk analysis, but this activity regularly requires two full-timers, that single person will quickly become a bottleneck and the team will always be late.

Assembling a team of all generalists is not always possible or even desirable. A reasonable middle ground is to have at least a couple of "specializing generalists" on the team and shift work to them as needed.

> I recently saw this pattern play out among the staff at a hotel, where I taught a course and stayed overnight. A few people specialized in front-desk services. Four others could both work the front desk and drive the shuttle. Another one dealt both with sales and with guests. The sales manager dealt with contracts as well as facilities and supplies. As the customer, I rarely had to wait for anything, whether a shuttle ride or an additional flipchart. Contrast this with most hotels, where staffers have narrow job descriptions and are sometimes prevented from crossing lines. There, if you need something, you must wait until a specialist or supervisor frees up.

A typical Agile team starts its Agile journey as a group of specialists, and its members naturally expect this state of affairs to continue. Some might be worried that sharing skills and responsibilities might diminish their individual contribution or compromise their job security. I've also seen the opposite, where team members enjoy the possibility — nowadays valued and encouraged — to widen their skill set and areas of contribution, especially via collaboration on real work rather than via formal instruction. This seems particularly true of teams that experience a high level of autonomy: members appreciate personal growth that also helps their team deliver better in the process.

Collaboration

A team generally has three options for processing a task:

+ Solo ownership: one person owns the task, and is the only person to work on it.

+ Hand-off: two or more people own portions of the task's life cycle.

+ Collaboration: two or more people own the task, and are responsible for completing it.

As discussed earlier, the first two are the most ubiquitous in the business world. Even when the workers are helpful and friendly toward each other, accountabilities are apportioned to individuals. This situation harks back to industrial-age beliefs around efficiency, specialization, and a separation of a person's work abilities from the rest of their humanity.

The Agile mind-set, originating in the knowledge-work era, espouses different beliefs both about the individuals and about the human systems they form. People *will* make mistakes, and the best way to mitigate that is with collaborative, self-organizing teams. Even without mistakes, teams may be smarter and more productive than the sum of their members. There can be magic in synergy, when artificial boundaries don't exist between colleagues.

These beliefs make *collaboration*, whose aspects of synergy and joint responsibility make it quite distinct from *cooperation*, highly desirable. It has several benefits:

✦ It allows ideas to grow, sometimes in unpredictable directions, since people think together.

✦ It builds the social fabric.

✦ It reduces delays, even when people focus on their specialties, because their "mini hand-offs" are immediate.

✦ It increases the quality of deliverables, since more people are involved in more stages of the work.

It doesn't follow, however, that teams should collaborate all day long. Indeed, some parts of work don't benefit significantly from collaboration, and not all the benefits may be equally important to you. Moreover, it can be exhausting, both physically and emotionally. A healthy, productive Agile team typically engages in considerable collaboration as well as some solo ownership and some hand-offs.

Collaboration is a matter of joint ownership of the results, not of being joined at the hip. It doesn't matter how much each person contributes. While it might involve working together from start to finish, it might also look like parallel work punctuated by frequent strategizing, analyzing, and cross-checking. It might involve two people ("pairing") or several ("mobbing" or "swarming"). Agile teams generally find it helpful to make collaboration part of their culture, or to base it on specific working agreements. For instance, on a team I managed long ago we had an agreement: "Nobody touches the database alone."

Given the popularity of Agile methods, you were probably familiar with the concepts of sprints, product owner, user stories, demos, and daily standup meetings before reading this book. These are useful ideas in some contexts; they may work for you, or not. My goal with this chapter is to give you and your team just enough detail on Agile choice-making so you can effectively design your own way of working and get started. Proceed with that work (which is the subject of chapter 8) as soon as possible, while the team's interest, attention, and goodwill are high.

SUPPLEMENTARY RESOURCE

Go to **AgileForNonSoftwareTeams.com** and download "Gil Broza's Process for Effective Feedback Requests."

Chapter 8
Design Your Initial Way of Working

Now is the time to **design your initial way of working**. Let's first unpack this phrase.

DESIGN: Determining a group's organization and its way of working is a system design activity that takes into account many factors, including human dynamics, constraints, and culture. Avoid the tempting shortcut of off-the-shelf methods, which may not fit your context. You can find examples from the field (and further evidence of the wide variety of Agile implementations) in the appendix.

INITIAL: Expect your methods and structure to evolve and improve. This expectation is in line with the Agile value of adaptation, and, more importantly, it is pragmatic. It's very hard (if not impossible) to design for best fit, and even if you could do so, conditions naturally change with time. You will be more successful by starting with a simple system,[1] so avoid the complexity of covering every eventuality. Document your choices and decisions to maximize shared understanding and alignment; however, don't turn anything into a new standard or template before you've proven its efficacy. Think of the initial design as your first in a series of gradual mini-experiments inside the bigger experiment with Agile.

WAY OF WORKING: You're attempting a mini-transformation of how your team works. That goes beyond replacing procedures, tools, and standards; it means making different choices about people and work. You should determine values, principles, and strategies before making changes to procedures, tools, and standards. Avoid the trap of "this is how things are done around here" and question your assumptions.

A point I made earlier bears repeating here. At least a dozen practices are in such common use among Agile teams, some even called "best practices," that you might be tempted to adopt them straightaway. Yet none of them will increase your Agility *at all* if your team doesn't also take on the mind-set that underlies those practices. For example:

✦ A task board won't provide valuable visibility, unless the team has true ownership of the board, motivation to keep it current, and the psychological safety to capture every task on it.

✦ A daily standup quickly becomes a boring status meeting unless the team feels safe and motivated to articulate meaningful impediments and collaborate on finishing work.

✦ Calling a group a "squad" or a "pod," or having them sit in a "collaborative space," won't make them a collaborating team unless they truly work toward shared objectives that require some interdependence.

By the same token: if you don't make software, don't copy practices from Agile software teams. That field uses technology to make technology, has had two decades to discover what works and what doesn't, and is a fast-moving target. If you're intrigued by a practice you see there, learn what Agile principles it fulfills, and if your implementation doesn't already manifest those principles, then fill that gap with your own creation.

For example, take the practice of automated testing: developers writing many tiny test programs to check that their "real" program works as intended. Reading about its intent will show you that it helps programmers work safely (they quickly know when they've broken something unintentionally) and that it reduces the cost of change (by preventing nasty surprises when making changes). If you then realize that your team isn't working as safely as they could, or that their work today makes tomorrow's changes costly, these will be the two issues to address. In another example, if having a frequent "demo" or "show and tell" meeting feels excessive or not valuable in your context, consider other ways to receive timely feedback from people who affect your work or are affected by it.

In chapter 4, you picked the target of your Agile experiment: a product, service, or solution you provide, or some other major responsibility or activity. At the highest level, you identified its customers, the outcomes it produces for them, and the value of those outcomes. This chapter covers the minimal steps to design an Agile-friendly way of working for that target that you can start using right away. These steps might take some time and span a few meetings or workshops, so make sure to follow them in sequence, collaborating with your team on every step. Although most professionals have very little experience in designing ways of working, I trust that if you invite them, engage them, and make their opinions count, they will participate usefully and give the resulting design an honest try.

Read this chapter fully before you act on its guidance. Doing so will give you the full picture of what you need to do, which will help you structure your meetings, conversations, or workshops. Moreover, because you're designing a *system* — not a linear thing — following this guidance in a single pass may not suffice. I've arranged the activities in the most efficient and sequential way I know, but be prepared to iterate on this process somewhat.

Choose Operating Principles

The other analysis you did in chapter 4 was of the values, constraints, and beliefs. Now, use this conceptual frame to choose your operating principles. In the next sections of this chapter, you'll use the principles to determine specific tactics, such as processes, practices, roles, and team touchpoints.

Draw your principles from these three sources:

✦ The Agile ones explained or mentioned in chapter 7

✦ Any you wish or need to retain from your current way of working

✦ Any others that you deem important

This will make for an interesting conversation with your team. Will you organize yourselves to produce outcomes easily, or around specialties? Will you forge a collaborative relationship with the customer, or expect a definitive set of requirements early on? Will you work in ways that keep the cost of change low, or make most choices early on and minimize change? Will you frequently and diligently check your work, or show it mostly at the end?

Every choice you make must agree with the chosen values, constraints, and beliefs. The closer those are to full congruence with the Agile set as described in this book, the more you'll be able to make use of the guidance of chapter 7. The farther those values and beliefs are from your current way of working, the less you'll retain from it. Try to get to a list that feels holistic and, more importantly, one that doesn't contain contradictions such as both team empowerment and extensive approvals, or impracticalities such as frequent feedback without breaking the work down.

Design the Workflow

A workflow, or process, describes what people do to get from idea to deliverable. In its most basic form, a workflow is a sequence of steps; in each step, people take the previous step's output, apply procedures and practices, and produce new output. Workflows may be simple sequences; they may diverge at points; they may have subworkflows; they may even have loops for iteration and improvement. For instance, consulting companies tend to have a basic workflow for turning prospects into clients, but that workflow has subcases depending on the type of client, the magnitude of work, and so forth.

You already know your current workflow well, whether it's documented in detail or "in your fingers." As you design your new workflow for greater Agility, many of the basic tasks will remain unchanged. It will be tempting, and seem reasonable, to retain most of your current workflow around those basic tasks. However, that will likely limit your Agility!

Even in the field that's been the most interested in Agile — software development — many organizations are still learning this lesson. For decades, the workflow was sequential and functional, with analysts passing requirements down to designers, developers passing code down to testers, and so on. This workflow *makes sense*, given the set of values and beliefs that reigned supreme — that of predictability and getting the solution right the first time. In truly Agile software teams, however, the workflow is very different. The steps are less sequential and more cyclical; teams break work down in different ways; even the concept of assigning specialized work to a single person is turned on its head.

The following 12 steps, phrased as questions, will help you design a workflow. Remember to keep it simple! Your process should implement your chosen principles, cover major cases reasonably well, and be easy to remember and follow. Don't try to cover every eventuality.

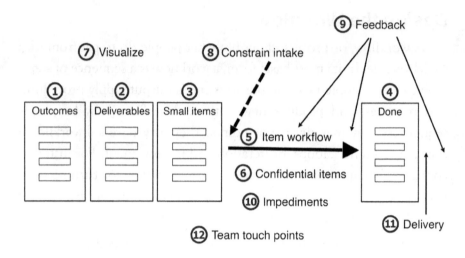

12 steps to designing your workflow

1. Who Will Manage the List of Outcomes, and How?

Outcomes are problems, needs, or goals, whether your customers', your organization's, or your own team's. Your list of outcomes, being the reason for having the team do their work, forms the starting point of a workflow. How will you manage that list?

Start by considering where outcomes come from and when the team first learns about them. If your company has annual or quarterly planning cycles, these probably determine outcomes that will require your team's involvement. If some customers manage their work as projects, their projects' inception stage is when most outcomes will be nailed down. Your list might also include recurring or cyclical outcomes, such as monthly or quarterly obligations. The team will offer innovative ideas, and customers may make new requests, anytime. There might be one-offs and future obligations, some of which could be time-bound.

Chances are, this is not a small list. Thus, the next step is to identify *who* would best decide which outcomes get addressed, and how they would make their choices. Your candidates should be oriented toward the customers, available, knowledgeable, confident, great communicators, and truly empowered to make those calls. Sounds demanding? It is. In Scrum, the most popular form of Agile, a single person is designated as the "product owner" to choose and sequence outcomes. In many non-software situations, that might be the group manager. If having a single person take responsibility for this matter is not a viable or desirable option in your case, consider having a small group of people instead; make sure they have a sound, transparent process for making decisions when facing disagreements. Eventually, this responsibility might be owned by the team, as long as there are clear tie-ins to business and customer needs.

Lastly, you need to decide how adaptive those deciders need to be: how often they should revisit/reprioritize the list of outcomes. That's not easy to determine; if the answer is "only at the beginning" or "every several months," you risk having the team produce suboptimal results. If the answer is "every week," that can send the team thrashing about.

2. Who Will Determine and Sequence the Deliverables, and How?

Given a desirable outcome, who would determine what solution/ deliverable the team should produce to accomplish it, and then would sequence the overall list of deliverables? And how would they do that?

This is not an obvious question to answer if you're not going with the old standby, the hierarchy. The Agile approach favors involving customers, subject matter experts, and some or all team members, rather than only senior people or managers. Including several people in the process might appear inefficient, but may lead to better results if done collaboratively and transparently. The same principles you're using now to design the workflow would guide their thinking about potential solutions/deliverables.

Nick Heling, Content Marketing Agile Coach, Red Hat:

"Our business unit stakeholders give my marketing group 'Point of View' documents, which are like mini-charters. We follow up with a collaborative workshop with the subject matter experts to draft the material together. This process also helps us learn a lot."

3. How Small Can You Make Work Items?

Chances are you have deliverables of all sizes and magnitudes. As explained in chapter 7, to achieve Agility you must decompose large deliverables into smaller work items, whose size and nature allow frequent value delivery, learning/feedback, risk mitigation, seizing opportunities, or enabling later value delivery. Many professionals who are new to Agile struggle with this skill, since they are used to decomposing work per the existing workflow and expertise distribution. For the same reason, some don't see the point of breaking work down the Agile way, or think of it as overhead, so they don't develop the skill.

Now is a good time to get some practice with your team. Pick a few real examples of work items, and try to decompose each one into smaller, meaningful items. You might have to decompose some of those into even smaller pieces. Try to get them down to a size at which, if the team doesn't experience any waiting or delays, they'll see progress on them every day.

This skill takes a great deal of practice, so if you're finding it difficult or alien, don't give up, and definitely don't let it stop you from considering the rest of Agile. On the other hand, if you're finding it easy, be careful not to overdo it; too many *tiny* tasks make for a very crowded board and increase administrative overhead.

4. What Does "Done" Mean?

As the team works on each item, they'll strive to get it to "done." Now, define this state: What does it mean — in your context — for a work item to be "done," finished, good to go? Which attributes or qualities should it have that will allow the team to move on to the next thing, not concerned about loose ends?

At this point, you only need to identify the criteria that apply to *all* items. Later on, as the team works on specific items, they will also need to know each item's specific "acceptance criteria." Those attributes or qualities indicate that the item indeed contributes to achieving the bigger outcome it came from.

For a simple universal example, take preparing a meal. The "done" checklist for any meal might include:

+ The table is set.

+ All the planned dishes are on the table, ready to eat.

Accomplishing the second criterion is where most of the work is; thus, when we break "preparing dinner" down into smaller tasks, we'll likely have one task per dish. The "done" criteria for any dish, whatever food it is, might include:

+ It's safe and ready to eat.

+ It's in an appropriate serving dish with appropriate utensils.

+ The quantity is sufficient.

+ There's nothing left to clean up or put away from the making of this dish.

In addition, each dish would have specific acceptance criteria. For example, a soup would have to be hot enough and its saltiness within a certain range for the diners to consume it.

---

5. What Should the Workflow of a Typical Work Item Be?

Now determine a simple workflow for a typical item. That is a sequence of states, starting from "ready" (sometimes called "to do," "next," "planned," or "committed") and reaching all the way to the item being "done." Thinking about examples of current, real work might help you elucidate the workflow, by asking "What do we do first? Then what? And then what?"

A business-to-business sales team evaluating their first attempt at determining the workflow. In this picture, they are conducting a "dry run," imagining what they would do with a specific potential customer, all the way from identifying a qualified lead at that company (left column) to signing a contract with it (right column).

Some teams make do with the simplest workflow, which has exactly three states: "Ready," "In progress," and "Done." A team will put an item in the first state when they've committed to seeing it through and understood it enough to prevent major surprises. When members actually start to work on it, they move it to "In progress"; when they've completed it, they move it to "Done." An item might get "blocked," meaning that something outside the team's control, such as an external review or approval, needs to happen before work on the item can resume. To reflect this situation, you might include a "Blocked" state in the workflow, or signal it with a special mark on affected items while they're "In progress."

The more states and signals your workflow has,* the better you'll see where work stalls or piles up. That information will come in handy when you attempt to streamline the process and achieve greater flow. With too many states, however, the administrative effort to accurately track each item's state becomes undesirable overhead. As well, a multi-state workflow might be unique to a particular class of work items, and then you might end up with many workflows. Beginning your Agile experiment with the basic three-state workflow described above can resolve both matters and reduce confusion. However, don't wait too long before you progress to a more granular representation of the workflow that can shed light on flow challenges.

If you successfully adopt the principle of breaking down work, you might realize a need for both a high-level workflow for deliverables and, inside it, a simple workflow for small items. For example, an Acquisitions team I'm working with has a nine-step workflow stretching from when they start looking at a company to the time they buy it. Some steps, such as negotiations and due diligence, involve significant work that they break down into smaller tasks whose workflow is the Ready - In Progress - Done described above.

Be careful about copying workflows from Agile books, online resources, or an electronic tool. They typically focus on software product development, where a single workflow covers most items, and is adapted to the complexities of that profession. It's usually some form of: develop the thing, get the product owner's acceptance for it, test it for defects, review the code with colleagues, document it. This might or might not be applicable in your situation.

---

* For example, if the work involves a lot of communication with third parties, you might add a state called "waiting for response"; or, if checking the deliverable requires two or more levels of inspection, you could separate those into distinct workflow steps.

6. How Will You Handle Sensitive or Confidential Work?

Transparency: everyone has access to all the artifacts, visibility into the status of every item, awareness of how decisions got made, and knowledge of what everyone is doing. Transparency enables Agility, and many teams make a conscious effort to maximize it. However, in your world, some work might be sensitive or confidential.

If team members may be fully transparent with each other but not with outsiders, you might solve this by holding team meetings and artifacts in restricted areas (whether in the real world or online). Nevertheless, provide nonmembers enough transparency into the team to allow trust and collaboration — or, more accurately, to prevent the mistrust and blame that may arise if they don't know what your team is up to.

If legitimate reasons prevent the members from being fully transparent with each other, now is the time to discuss what kinds of work are confidential, who gets involved, and to what extent. Such work items might be too few and far between to affect your overall process. Otherwise, discuss a reasonable way for dealing with them. Likely, the existence of confidential work is not a secret, while the details of specific items are in fact secret; if so, a simple solution could be to represent such work as a task titled "Confidential" and tagged with the people working on it. The people in charge of a confidential task would manage it and its flow privately. This way, everyone on the team has visibility into everyone's workload and constraints without necessarily being privy to sensitive details.

7. How Will You Visualize the Work?

In the early days of an Agile team, boards and workflows evolve quickly, so start simple. When a team is located in one area, sticky notes on a wall/window/whiteboard tend to be the visualization mode that's easiest to adopt and cheapest to adapt. Each note provides minimally necessary information about a single work item, such as its heading, who it's for (if not obvious), any date expectations, and which team members are currently working on it. When necessary, the notes reference electronic documents that contain further detail. The alternative to pen and paper — installing an Agile management tool and configuring it for your specifics — tends to take longer to set up and often dissuades people from evolving the workflow (because they have to update all the items every time it changes). If your team is dispersed, or frequently works from home, you'll probably have to start with an electronic tool. Plenty of free tools exist that you can try out, and if you don't like any of them, use a spreadsheet.

Since you're just starting and experimenting, capture (on sticky notes or in an electronic tool) only the items that are coming up in the next few days or weeks. This will make the work clearer to see and will reduce the cost of modifying items if you change the workflow's design — which will happen soon.

Breanna Ramos, HR Associate, TechSmith:

"We tried using a board for every project, and that was too much. Then we tried a single board for all the projects, and that was hard to use too. Now we use a single board, with a swim lane for each person, and color-coding for any project work items."

Electronic tools are susceptible to the "out of sight, out of mind" risk: many teams neglect to update them in a timely fashion, so their boards lose their utility as a work management tool. If you see this happen, make it a priority for yourself to help the team build the *habit* of reflecting their work's state on the board. If they consider it administrative overhead, contrast it with the gain in both alignment and visibility into what's important.

8. How Will You Constrain the Team's Work Intake?

As explained in chapter 7, the team should intentionally limit how many small items they take on at any given time. For those new to Agile or to Lean, who often believe that multitasking increases productivity without compromising quality, constraining intake as a way to increase flow seems a strange concept. Thus, many use it ineffectually or not at all. For instance, they use sprints (iterations) that are several weeks long or have WIP limits that allow considerable multitasking.

Discuss this matter with the team now; build familiarity with the concept of self-constraining, and try to get an agreement about limiting intake. If you can't, let it go, and don't worry too much about it in the early days. Regardless, monitor the extent of work in progress and be on the lookout for the consequences, such as overloaded team members, a lot of work started but not finished, or too much solo work. If any of these consequences occur, arrange opportunities for learning and reflection about them.

If you're applying Agile to two or more different kinds of work, such as both discretionary projects and business-as-usual (BAU), the team will need a strategy for choosing next tasks. The strategy should take into account their different commitments, constraints, and consequences.

Claire Brown, Agile Coach supporting three Enterprise Risk Strategy teams:

"Each team's board is divided by a horizontal line. Above it is all the BAU work that they must do, and below is all discretionary work, such as projects and improvements. In their planning event every two weeks, they agree on a motivating goal to keep them focused, and populate their boards with what they believe is achievable for the two weeks ahead. Every day when they meet at the board, they discuss and commit to BAU items first, and whenever they have spare capacity, they commit to items from below the line, always keeping their eyes on the previously agreed goal."

9. Which Feedback Loops Should You Have for Work Content?

A basic strategy in Agile is to rely extensively on feedback for getting the work right when you don't (or can't) have all the answers up front. Here are some questions to ponder with the team:

+ What kinds of questions should we ask, and of whom, to validate that we're on a right track?*

+ How frequently, or at what points, should we be asking those questions? What's practical?

+ Which channels of communication for feedback are both effective and realistic?

+ What sort of feedback should we seek from each other, before we go outside for more?

+ What needs to happen for feedback-givers to feel safe enough to tell us what they really think?

+ What needs to happen for feedback-receivers to feel safe both requesting it and hearing it?

+ How will we act if we receive feedback that invalidates a lot of what we did?

A partial answer to the first three questions comes from the Scrum framework. At the end of every sprint — a cycle of work, usually one or two weeks long — the team gathers for a sprint review meeting. At that meeting (colloquially referred to as the "demo" or "show and tell"), customers and stakeholders get to see what the team produced or learned in that sprint that relates to outcomes and solutions they care about. The review meeting is thus a regular, predictable opportunity for soliciting feedback and discussing it collaboratively, face-to-face. It's particularly suitable for teams in which everyone works on the same

---

* Notice I didn't say "*the* right track"; there may be more than one way to accomplish an outcome.

evolving product and at a discernible cadence. It might be useful for you; it might also feel awkward if your team does conceptually different things for different stakeholders. In that case, be creative, and feel free to solicit feedback in focused one-on-one settings instead.

Nick Heling:

"My team creates marketing content, particularly content strategy, to support products and solutions. We used to demo our work to senior leaders; we've switched to demoing, multiple times per sprint, to the stakeholders who happen to be associated with that sprint's objective."

A special case of the feedback loop is *approval*. Make a list: At which points in your current workflow does work wait for the approval of a supervisor, manager, or expert before it proceeds to the next step? For each point, make sure you articulate the purpose of the approval, and also attempt to calculate both the average delay it creates and the potential negative effect on the team's engagement and motivation. If either is high, consider applying these alternate means, all of which ensure that more than a single pair of eyes examine a deliverable:

+ Collaboration: two or more team members take joint ownership of producing the deliverable.

+ Peer review: a peer, who wasn't involved in the work, inspects it and provides feedback.

+ Early and frequent feedback from customers: the workers are responsible for soliciting such feedback from their customers and then acting on it.

+ Acceptance criteria: before starting work, elicit a checklist of criteria the deliverable has to satisfy in order to be acceptable to the customer.

10. What Sort of Impediments Do You Foresee, and What Will You Do About Them?

Even with proper organization and process, a team will experience impediments (obstacles) to their progress or productivity. Teams that are trying Agile for the first time experience them almost daily... without realizing it! Many situations that impede Agility go unnoticed because, pre-Agile, they were normal reality. Thus, a necessary condition for eventually becoming a strong Agile team is adopting the habit of noticing impediments and then taking action. To start building this habit with your team, generate a short list of likely impediments and reasonable responses. Use the following as prompts:

+ Some impediments are due to workflow or team design. For instance, work can't be completed or moved to the next stage, work can't be started due to missing information, a deliverable is waiting for rework, or a team member is waiting to hear back from an expert or from someone outside the team.

+ Some impediments arise simply from working within an organization. For example, a sign-off is needed, organizational procedures complicate or delay planning, or critical stakeholders are too busy to give the team feedback.

+ Many impediments have to do with the team's and organization's being made up of humans. Examples include loss of focus due to excessive interruptions, incorrect progress caused by faulty assumptions or partial communication, and missed actions ("dropped balls").

As you discuss possible responses to those impediments, you might notice their common denominator: *talking to people*. Actually talking, not just sending messages. For instance, if another department's process is creating long delays for your team, picking up the phone and explaining why the team needs a quick turnaround may be all that's needed. If the problems repeat themselves or you start seeing patterns, you'll probably need to convene a few people to discuss a process change or a new working agreement. Remember, it's people who made all the processes, so it's people who can change them. Never assume that if an impediment has to do with someone outside the team, you're stuck with it.

11. How Will You Get Finished Deliverables into Customers' Hands?

The team may be diligent about its work, and finish items without delay, but the value is not there if the team doesn't deliver the finished goods, or if the customers don't take delivery. You'll have seen this if you've ever paid for a specialty drink at a coffee shop and they forgot to tell you it's ready, or you've bought a fancy gadget and it's still languishing in its package.

Review the types of deliverables you produce and decide:

+ When will you deliver each: When it's ready, when you've amassed a few, or during specific windows of opportunity?

+ In what form will they be, to make them immediately usable to the customers?

+ How will the customers know they're ready: Phone call, email, automated notification, some other signal?

+ How will you know that they've actually taken delivery and benefited from the results: Will you follow up, or will they commit to circling back with you?

Different kinds of deliverables may well get different treatment.

12. Which Touchpoints Will the Team Have?

We've looked at managing outcomes, solutions, and work intake. Technically, you can perform each activity opportunistically, anytime there's new information or a decision to make. You might also decide to do them cyclically, on a cadence. For instance, many Agile teams work in sprints or iterations — consecutive time-boxes of fixed size, typically one week or two — and have a planning meeting at the beginning of each. Many new-to-Agile teams find that this kind of regular cadence ("heartbeat") helps them create good habits. Whatever you choose, if you value adaptation and responsiveness, don't go too long between opportunities to replenish the team's list of upcoming work.

We've also looked at the small-item workflow. Many Agile teams find it useful to have a quick daily touchpoint, known as the daily standup, for timely micro-planning.* Collaboratively, they determine what they'll do to finish what's in progress, what they'll do about new information, how they'll unhinge blocked items, what they'll start after those items are done, and how to take advantage of spare capacity. When run as a meeting by the team and for the team, rather than as a status meeting where people report progress to a manager, the daily standup moves work along *and* helps build team muscle and engagement. For example, it often helps early-stage teams realize how frequently members wait for each other, thus prompting improvements to the workflow.

SUPPLEMENTARY RESOURCE: Download "Tips for an Effective Daily Standup / Touchpoint" from the book's companion website, **AgileForNonSoftwareTeams.com**.

The Agile principle of continuous improvement usually gives rise to another team touchpoint known as the retrospective. In this meeting, the team draws lessons from recent experiences to improve their workflow and teamwork. Retrospectives require psychological safety (meaning that people can discuss potentially sensitive matters freely) and sufficient frequency to be effective. If you hold these team events at regular short intervals, such as every couple of weeks, folks know they never go long before discussing their issues in a safe space, which helps prevent small problems from becoming big ones. If the team uses iterations/sprints, it usually works well to have the retrospective as the

---

* A typical meeting should be 5 to 15 minutes long. To be efficient, it should focus on matters that concern the entire team; after it's over, small groups proceed to discuss matters that interest only them.

closing event of the sprint. Decide now when you'll have them; chapter 9 provides more detail about conducting them usefully.

The above are guaranteed team events: even if most of the time members work in relative isolation (not great!), at least during these meetings they get to review matters and decide together. You don't have to make a ceremony out of these meetings; in fact, *do not* call them ceremonies, as that would be valuing process over people. Do make sure they're a safe space where healthy conversations and collaboration take place. If you see the need for additional team touchpoints, set them up.

Once the team starts the experiment and these touchpoints become a regular part of their schedule, apply the same principles you chose at the beginning of this chapter to the process of each meeting. For example, if you chose visualization: capture key input and decisions visually. If you chose collaboration: structure the activities to allow ideas to build on each other. If you chose cost of change: when contemplating certain decisions, such as work item breakdown or a workflow change, discuss the cost of changing or undoing them.

Structure the Team

Membership

As you embark on your Agile journey, the *work* will remain virtually unchanged, and most likely so will the *team*; the biggest change will be to the team's ways of doing that work. However, the success of that change will also depend on the team's makeup. That's because the Agile kind of teamwork — semi-autonomous, cross-functional with extensive collaboration and cooperation, obsessing over finishing and frequent feedback — is a new experience to most people. Some don't care for it; some don't want to experience it with specific colleagues; some have too-narrow skills to use it effectively. Your pre-Agile parameters for teamwork might not have required a high level of interdependence and mutual accountability to float such issues.

Here are 10 criteria I use to assess a team's likelihood of success as an Agile team. Consider the team you have now, or the team you intend to form; score each criterion with 0, 0.5, or 1, based on the extent to which the team's membership as a whole satisfies that criterion, or could satisfy it if given attention and support. Then total the numbers. Remember: you're scoring the team as a unit, not individuals.

- Communication: Can members communicate easily and effectively? (Would relocation, tooling, or schedule coordination help?)

- Relationships: Do they *all* get along, or have the potential for creating good working relationships?

- Equality: If the team has contractors, freelancers, part-timers, or interns, are they treated as equal members, and do *all* members feel similar ownership of the deliverables?

- Collaboration: Is there (or can there be) a high level of collaboration among members, including across traditional or functional divides?

- Motivation: Are they motivated to do this team's particular work?

- Leadership: Is there enough supportive, enabling, and empathetic leadership on the team (whether dedicated or shared) to help them succeed as an Agile team?

- Finishing: Can they finish valuable deliverables without requiring (or with quick access to) people from outside the team?

- Delays: When the team starts work they can finish on their own, can they do so without internal delays and bottlenecks?

- System: Can *other teams* proceed unhindered if they have only limited access to members of this team?

- Change: Does this team voluntarily seek and apply feedback, learn as much as they can, and improve their work? (Or, could it become the norm?)

SUPPLEMENTARY RESOURCE: Download "10 Team Design Criteria Worksheet" from the book's companion website, **AgileForNonSoftwareTeams.com**.

This checklist is not scientific, objective, or precise. Yet, if your total score for the team is under 7, consider that a risk; even if they try to correctly apply everything in this book, their efforts would be hamstrung because they wouldn't or couldn't act as a true, focused team.

If you're seeing such a risk, but can't change the team's membership, note your thoughts and insights from this assessment and watch for red flags during the first few months. Alternatively, you might be able to pilot your use of Agile with a subset of the existing team, focused on a subset of outcomes or work types, that is more likely to succeed.

One possible reason for a low score is that the team is too small or too large. A small team may not be able to complete deliverables that matter to customers. Large teams have different challenges and risks, such as the formation of cliques and rifts, and the shared team objectives mushrooming into several different objectives. There's no universally correct answer to the question "How large is too large?" as it depends on many variables. For example, a large team might score low on the interpersonal criteria above, while scoring higher on the delay- and dependencies-related ones because of their greater skill-set. If the team feels too large, consider whether you should instead have two or three smaller teams, each focused on a customer segment, work type, or set of objectives.

Another common root cause of a low score is team members' availability. While not everyone needs to be 100% dedicated to the team, having lower availability and incompatible or unpredictable schedules will hamper their success. The first sign of trouble will be delays, as people wait for others to free up from other obligations, especially if those others are specialists. The second sign will be avoidance of collaboration, as people start assuming it's too hard to bring about. The team might even want to modify the board to focus on individuals' tasks instead of on team deliverables. The team will not be experiencing much Agility at this point.

If low availability is a result of having each member be responsible for different products or deliverables, consider making the whole team responsible for all the products. Each member might remain the specialist in their particular domain, but is no longer the sole worker or owner of it. This team would continuously self-organize around whichever products and outcomes are the priority. Alternatively, help the team block chunks of time (the same ones every week if possible) to work as a whole team on a given product, as described in the example on page 40.

The skill and expertise distribution in your team might make shared ownership and collaboration appear unlikely. That is still a legitimate starting point, and the team is not doomed. Nevertheless, assess each expertise: Is it always vital for the work, is it needed only at certain junctures, or will general competence suffice? Will the available supply of that expertise pose an impediment, and should the team get more of it? What kind of investment in skill building would be worth it? This matter deserves a strategic response, but be careful: it can be touchy. On one hand, many people love to widen or deepen their skill set; on the other hand, fears around implicit competition, identity, and job security abound.

In conversations with clients, I often hear the belief that for people to collaborate on a task, all of them must specialize in its subject matter (and by consequence, little collaboration will take place because folks specialize in different areas). I consider that a limiting belief, and I help people reconsider it situationally with this question: "Which aspects of the task could benefit from collaboration even if only one of the participants specializes in the task?" Whatever the task is, the answers often include: seeing more of the big picture, identifying missed cases and opportunities, considering what-ifs, catching mistakes, and sharing knowledge.

Another possible constraint on your team design may arise when some members are required as product owners or subject matter experts for other Agile teams, such as technology development teams. In the simplest case, it's always the same people and they are required to be away all the time. Matters get more complicated when you're short on staff, need backup for the "away" people, or can't forecast when they'll be needed. This can easily throw off the rest of the team's work. You might need to get creative about the team structure, even to the extent of not including the "away" in the Agile team you're forming (though they'll keep their reporting line). However you design the team structure, you'll need to establish clear policies regarding work that doesn't serve the team itself, such as how to manage demand and how to visualize it.

A hidden assumption in this section is that the team's membership stays constant throughout the experiment. That is critical! Even if over the long term you expect some movement of people between teams, prevent it as much as possible during this vital learning period. So much Agile success relies on building trusting, collaborative relationships among colleagues. It takes weeks, even months — give them a chance to do it.

Roles and Responsibilities

Make a list of the various responsibilities (activities) the team requires for working well, whether those responsibilities are shared or only one person's. Since the fundamental work itself won't likely change with the use of Agile, you should find it quick and easy to produce the list. Now, add to it any responsibilities you've noticed in this chapter so far, such as managing intake, proposing solutions, and processing feedback. Then add the following responsibilities:

LOOK AFTER THE WAY OF WORKING. Agile teams expect to gradually improve how they work, but realistically, few people notice process or care for it. Make process stewardship an explicit responsibility.

LOOK AFTER TEAM HEALTH. The health of the human system — how individuals are and how they interact in the context of getting work done — is critical, and must receive someone's attention.

REMOVE IMPEDIMENTS. Expecting every team member to notice extrinsic problems is not always realistic, and having them address those problems may eat into the focus they need to do their work. Therefore, having impediment management as an explicit responsibility of one or more people may improve the *team's* performance.

FACILITATE TEAM MEETINGS. Effective Agile meetings have high levels of communication, collaboration, self-organization, and consensus.* Achieving that usually requires someone to take the role of facilitator, leading the *process* of the meeting so that it achieves its outcome with maximum application of these principles.[2]

People may now sign up for these responsibilities, with no official designation of roles. Alternatively, you can determine roles, map the responsibilities to them, and assign the roles to people. Since Agile favors shared ownership and team proactivity (agency), responsibilities don't always pertain to single roles, and it's not uncommon to see teams with fuzzy roles because everyone does most of everything. That said, the following set of three roles is almost a canonical form or baseline:

1. A single "product owner" is responsible at least for managing and prioritizing outcomes, clarifying stakeholders' requests, sequencing deliverables, and giving feedback on them once produced.

2. A team leader, acting as a servant leader, is responsible at least for looking after the team's health and way of working, keeping track of the work, removing impediments to flow, and facilitating meetings.

3. Every other worker (nonmanagement) is a "team member."

---

* Consensus does not mean 100% agreement or having the same opinion. When a group reaches consensus on a suggestion, it means all the members agree to support it so that the group can move ahead, even if some individuals may have different preferences.

This arrangement is particularly valuable because it gives a home to each critical concern — team, outcomes, and work — without creating a potential conflict of interest. It is also flat: nobody is anybody's boss,* so members are more likely to bring their best selves to work *and* to collaborate. If this arrangement works for you, give it a try (your situation might call for additional roles). Otherwise, design some other combination as a starting point. Just keep things simple.

What about managers, you might ask? Agile teams still have them, but their role, and particularly how they show up, are a bit different. Agile managers continue to look after people and their career development, staffing and budgeting, organizational capabilities, escalation, and strategy. One key responsibility they typically shed in the move to Agile is that of assigning tasks and following up on status; as a matter of autonomy and self-organization, the team typically does that for themselves. Which additional responsibilities an Agile manager will have depends on the context; perhaps in your case, the manager is best placed to manage intake, to sequence outcomes, or to look after team health. As long as the team feels enough psychological safety and doesn't wait to be told each next step, that could be a fine starting point.

Keep in mind that all the above are *roles*, not jobs. For now, don't change formal titles, job descriptions, reporting lines, authority levels, or compensation. Such changes would create unnecessary tension, and possibly complicate matters if the experiment runs into trouble. Leave official HR changes for later, once you have an arrangement that works.

Space

In environments where people have their own work and don't need to interact much with peers, their desk location or work-from-home situation isn't a big issue. In Agile teams, however, the level of interaction

---

* Agile favors flat structures, but 99.99% of real-world Agile teams operate inside an organizational hierarchy or an uneven power structure. That does not invalidate Agile's applicability, but it may make it harder.

and codependence is fairly high, so distances and the physical environment matter. Colleagues sitting very close to each other are more likely to collaborate, to notice mistakes sooner, and to build relationships that will help them in difficult times. By contrast, colleagues who don't sit within earshot of each other will either have to try harder to achieve those effects, or they simply won't bother, effectively maintaining a higher level of individual task ownership.

If your team is not used to having a collaborative space, don't force one on them. People get very attached to their desk or office, and are likely to perceive a triple loss of space, privacy, and control if compelled to relocate to an open area. Let them choose their workspace configuration, and support them in evolving it over time (usually by discussing it in retrospectives). Consider the following ideas to help their deliberations:

+ If they are open to "moving in together," they can treat that as an experiment. Make it possible to restore their current setup if the experiment doesn't work out.

+ You may not have to build out a new space per the company standard. Many Agile teams do just fine by taking over a room containing a big table or several smaller ones. This is especially easy if they have laptops. With luck, the room will have some wall space on which they can visualize their work. If the space works out, it can be upgraded to the standard.

+ A team that is strapped for space can stay where they are, but they would benefit from having access to a meeting room (always the same one) for their team touchpoints and shared artifacts.

+ A team that's dispersed across an office, and can't move to a collaborative space of their own, might be able to move closer together if they switch desks with others not on their team.

If colocation is a real possibility, but you're noticing that team members are stonewalling workspace discussions, shooting down colocation options, or going for digital collaboration instead, that's a red flag.

Whenever I've seen this happen, they were resisting the very idea of Agile teamwork while not being explicit about it. Rather than give in to their objections or compel them to colocate, reflect on what you're observing, or get to the bottom of the matter in private conversations. Your entire Agile experiment could be at risk.

> Phew! If you feel this was a lot, I would agree with you. Designing a way of working is no small feat, and certainly not something you can effectively copy–paste from elsewhere. Doing the above with clients often takes me a day or two, yet the potential gains are huge. Ideally, the team will get started very soon (otherwise, the whole exercise won't feel real). Before the first official day, be sure to read the next chapter.

SUPPLEMENTARY RESOURCE

Go to **AgileForNonSoftwareTeams.com** and download "Tips for an Effective Daily Standup / Touchpoint" and "10 Team Design Criteria Worksheet."

Chapter 9

Support the Team During the First Few Months

Remember the Satir Change Model? Planning and preparation won't help you sidestep the chaos stage, but they *will* mitigate its effects and duration. If you followed all my guidance in the previous chapter, then this is as much as you can reasonably prepare. You have given thought to all important elements. If you're not feeling confident about your initial way of working, or are concerned that it's not complete, rest assured: you've handled the most important success factor, which is to have a customized starting point. This chapter provides guidance for day one and all through the first few months, to help everyone get the hang of Agile with minimal thrashing and trouble.

Start with a Kick-off

Even if you're trying Agile on only one type of work, chances are your new way of working will be quite different from the current one. Call attention to the significance and extent of the change by *kicking off* the experiment.

A kick-off is a team meeting that marks a formal start. It's especially poignant for a team whose work, week to week and month to month, is somewhat routine. A kick-off might take anywhere from 30 minutes, if the team is already familiar with most of the content, to two hours, if they need to build shared understanding. More than a notional transfer of information, a successful kick-off touches people emotionally; therefore, keys to success include compelling delivery, confidence, and engagement. You might want to use the following structure:

1. Provide context. Bring the charter you drafted in chapter 4. Review it together, emphasizing what you're hoping the team will achieve for themselves, their customers, and the organization.

2. Reiterate the motivation for a different way of working. Take care not to portray the existing way in a negative light, because it's been the best that people knew so far.

3. Remind people of how the new way was designed.

4. Describe the initial workflow and structure. Make sure everyone understands it the same way, and demonstrate how it manifests the chosen values and principles.

5. Reiterate that it's an experiment. Explain what's changing, what's not, and the strategy regarding preexisting obligations.

6. Answer any open questions, especially those that indicate concern or anxiety.

7. Answer "what if" questions ("What if this doesn't work?" "What if we hate it?" "What if senior management doesn't like it?").

8. Gain commitment. Let everyone involved in the experiment commit, publicly, to giving it an honest try.

If the entire team has participated in the design process, they will already know all the above, and the kick-off will be little more than a brief official start. Otherwise, this is your opportunity to catch everyone up on decisions, answer questions, and secure their commitment. Key to that is to make the experiment *safe* (especially in steps 5-7). Nobody should be worrying about their job, title, compensation, performance review, or desk space. Choose your words and promises well to ensure safety.

Finish Small Valuable Work Together

As the team works, expect to see these dynamics play out:

+ Some members will strive to follow the process exactly as designed, while others will "color outside the lines."

+ When an issue arises that the workflow didn't account for, some people will address it based on the chosen design principles. Others will invoke principles that they are comfortable with (for example, you might hear "In my previous company, they drilled into us: 'measure twice, cut once'"). Yet others will wait for a ruling from you.

+ Some members will look online for additional advice or "best practices" and wonder, privately or publicly, why the team is not using them.

These dynamics are inevitable because people want to be successful, and since they are not clones, they will have different approaches to the same situations. Some prefer proven procedures, while others prefer having options; where some see problems, others see opportunities; some want to learn from a given situation, while others want to just move on. While these dynamics can expand the options, more often they create noise that makes it hard for the team to succeed *together*.

The solution is to be explicit and relentless about a shared mind-set: values, beliefs, and principles. You've articulated them during the design; people have committed to them; now, make sure they act accordingly. Not with rewards and punishments, but with empathy, observations, listening, coaching, reminders, and reasoning.

It won't be easy, because those are *lists*. People struggle to remember new values and principles when they adopt them, and struggle to artic-ulate them once they become second nature. To make it easier, consider using hand-drawn posters and mantras. Posters — with pictures, icons, or words — will provide a visual reminder. Mantras are short phrases that you can use in conversations.

A mantra I like using with teams is: *finish small valuable work together* (FSVWT). Even if they apply it only some of the time, it's still effective. Clearly, this mantra reinforces key Agile ideas: finishing, value, and collab-oration. It suppresses behavioral patterns that hinder Agility, such as silo-ing (individual specialization and task ownership) and overemphasizing the process. And the built-in frequent wins are a powerful, simple catalyst to team growth. Finishing something valuable provides visible evidence of success, and when that something is small, success is quick to arrive.

SUPPLEMENTARY RESOURCE: Download "Collaboration Etiquette Posters" from the book's companion website, **AgileForNonSoftwareTeams.com**.

It's the "small" portion of FSVWT that will be tricky. As chapter 7 explained, *how* you make the work small is important. Breaking work down to a sequence of hand-offs between specialists might be familiar and easy, but for Agility, choose tasks that provide value, increase learn-ing, allow feedback, mitigate risk, seize an opportunity, or control the cost of change. For most team members, doing so will be unfamiliar; it might seem like pointless administrative overhead; and they might be worried that showing partial, emerging deliverables would reflect badly on them. Be patient, work collaboratively, and make it safe to try. It takes most people weeks to build this skill.

Teams new to Agile or to teamwork seem to have a grace period of two to three months during which people will give each other and their new methods a chance. Past that period, they are more likely to devolve into groups of individuals "doing their parts." During the grace period, frequently remind the team to FSVWT, and they'll have a much higher likelihood of success as a team.

Make Working Agreements

No amount of upfront workflow design and planning can cover every situation that your team will encounter.[1] Even the Project Management Body of Knowledge, which has been captured in several thick tomes,[2] cannot address every situation encountered by real-life practitioners.

As mentioned before, intentionality and explicitness of mind-set will help everyone respond consistently to situations that arise. The team should add a few high-impact working agreements, which codify important matters they never considered or express desired behaviors that don't occur regularly enough. In most teams, agreements relate to interpersonal matters such as collaboration, transparency, decision-making, feedback, and keeping each other informed. Examples from teams I've worked with include:

- ✦ Collaboration and interactions. "Give help when asked." "If you're not learning or contributing in a meeting, feel free to go do something else that's useful." "If your task has a high potential for errors, whoever you ask to collaborate with you must say yes." "One language in the office." "No headphones."

- ✦ Behavioral expectations. "If a work item is not on the team board, we don't do it." "Work on team stuff only in the team space."

- ✦ Decision-making. "At least three people must participate in making high-level design decisions." "If you're not in the room, you accept the group's decision. If you can't attend, someone may speak for you."

Agreements should be written down, since human memory can be rather plastic and misleading. The act of writing an agreement down is a chance for clarification and refinement. Post written agreements visibly to make them a nagging-free, accessible reminder, something they can never be if buried in some electronic tool.

The word "agreement" is well-chosen, connoting a more informal convention than "bylaw" or "rule," and more humility and context-awareness than "best practice." Agreements remain in effect until the team wants to change them. Simple, reasonable, workable agreements are easier to put in place than perfect ones. Anyone can suggest them, and they require everyone's commitment to become binding. Managers should not force agreements on a team, but may point out the need for them.

Pat Reed, Senior Director, Gap, Inc.:

"One of our teams came up with a 'wheel of shame' to deal with the inevitable violation of working agreements. The transgressor would have to spin the wheel of shame and carry out whichever 'punishment' the dial landed on, which usually involved having to do something silly like wear a silly hat or treat the rest of the team to ice cream. It was a surprisingly effective and fun way to defuse problem behavior and enhance the team's sense of cohesion."

Stabilize the System

If you think of your team's work management system as having demand on one side and supply on the other, you'll want to create *balance* (good flow) between those two end-points. That will increase its reliability, which will support overall business performance and agility.

Visualizing the work is critical for understanding, and thereby managing, its flow. When you consistently capture all the work in a visual manner, it becomes easy to detect forms of imbalance: more items getting started than finished, items piling up someplace along the workflow, or items getting blocked. And, when you calculate and graph how long the team has been taking to process work items,[3] it becomes easy to see trends and variance. Imbalance and high variance generally indicate that the system, through which the work flows, is unstable. In chapter 7 you read about, and in chapter 8 you used, two basic principles that improve flow: constraining work intake and getting to "done" (focusing on finishing what's started). Below are four additional ideas to stabilize your system.[4]

PULL WORK INTO WIP-LIMITED WORKFLOW STAGES. Set a work-in-progress limit on *every* intermediate stage, and take work ("pull") into each stage only if its limit allows. For example, imagine your workflow is a simple Ready - Doing - Checking - Done, and that all five team members can process work in "Doing" but only two of them may do "Checking." You might experiment with a limit of four items on the Doing column and a limit of two items on the Checking column. If the Doing column is full (that is, the team is currently "doing" four items), they won't take on another one. Instead, once the Checking column drops to one item or to none and an item in Doing is finished, the team may move ("pull") it to the Checking column. Try this for a short while and, based on the results, consider tweaking the limits.

MANAGE CHRONIC WAITS AND BLOCKERS. Often, the tasks that throw systems off-balance are not the labor-intensive ones, but the ones that incur delays and blockages. Nothing useful happens while they wait in some queue, and since people don't want to be idle, they start working on other items and subsequently get themselves into the trouble described earlier. So, look for repeated delays and blockages that are due to your workflow design or to organizational policies, and see how you can mitigate them. For example, see chapter 8 for alternatives to approvals.

CLEAR TEMPORARY CONGESTION. Visualization will help you trace erratic flow to a specific root cause: too much demand is hitting a part of the workflow. (For example, think of live concerts; the food stands are not usually busy, but have long lines during intermissions.) If you see work pile up in one column, avoid pushing more work into that column or starting other work. Remember, optimizing for keeping everyone fully loaded will create bottlenecks, especially at the specialists, and the team won't be able to deliver finished results fast enough or reliably enough. Instead, shift efforts toward clearing the congestion. One form of increasing capacity this way is the "all hands on deck" strategy.

"Before and after" pictures of a seven-person team's board. In this picture, the team had just set up their board, and they're putting on it every item they were working on or planning to. Notice their high WIP, both overall and in three mid-workflow columns.

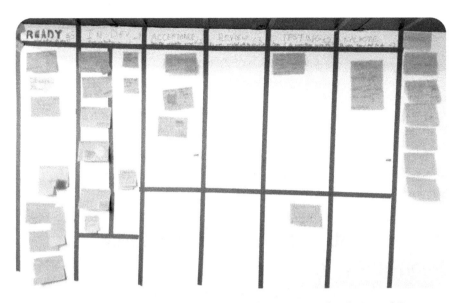

Two weeks later, the team had cleared the congestion in two of the three columns — essentially, they got to "done" on every item whose state was already advanced — and had reduced the number of items in the third column to its WIP limit.

DETERMINE HOW TO HANDLE RUSH JOBS AND EMERGENCIES. These kinds of work delay other important work, for several reasons. The obvious reason is that they take time away from the team; less obviously, by disrupting flow and causing expensive task switching, they sap even more time and attention. Some rushes and emergencies are real and justify a response; one popular mechanism is to set aside a little team capacity that may be immediately used for expediting work. That capacity might be shared by the team or provided by a specific person on rotation. This solution is analogous to the shoulder on a highway: a usable lane that is kept empty except for emergencies. Some emergencies, though, are false and ought to be funneled through the regular workflow. If you set clear and meaningful "service level expectations" for normal work and achieve them, your customers and stakeholders will likely treat fewer items as emergencies.[5]

One important manifestation of the "people first" value is *sustainable pace*: the team should be able to maintain its pace indefinitely. This is a necessary condition for having a stable system that has a predictable, reliable rate of value delivery as well as the capability for long-term performance. Perhaps more important, stable systems also prevent the drawbacks of *unsustainable* pace: lower-quality work, burnout, sickness, and turnover. Make sure the team understands their capacity[6] and doesn't accidentally (or intentionally!) overcommit themselves on a regular basis.

Watch for Attitudes and Behaviors that Hamper Agility

When human beings try to operate with a different mind-set, they're prone to exhibiting attitudes and behaviors that have served them so far, but don't align to the new mind-set. That's natural. Your team will have to notice and manage their bounce-backs for several months. Being part of an organization will present an extra challenge for them during this time: they will continue interacting with others, especially managers and stakeholders, who are not part of the change and thus *will* continue to behave as they have done so far.

Be on the lookout for attitudes and behaviors — anyone's, *including your own!* — that undermine the efforts to change the team's way of working. Here are several examples, which I've seen again and again in Agile transformations, and suggestions for how you might respond to them.

In planning, the team is looking at decomposing a large work item, and the product owner/stakeholder/manager says, "We need the whole thing anyway, so don't bother splitting it — there's no value in that." The consequence of doing so? Delaying value, slowing feedback, and making it harder to change course. Even if the customer wouldn't take delivery of a part of the deliverable, splitting it into a sequence of a few meaningful pieces will allow earlier feedback and course correction.

In planning: "Task X is in such-and-such area, which is Hayley's speciality. Hayley, you'll do that one." While it's reasonable to expect a specialist to perform "their" tasks better and faster, that won't be the result if the specialist is overloaded and can't get to them soon enough. Consistently assigning tasks to overloaded specialists is the best way to create delays and hurt teamwork, and it's a vicious cycle. Instead, invest in spreading knowledge and skills around in order to limit dependency on specialists to the really hard cases.

The team is working on task Y, and manager/stakeholder asks them: "When will you be done?" This question makes sense only when the workers have only that task to work on and its level of complexity makes estimation viable. A safer, more empowering alternative, is: "Can you give me a range for how long you might need to complete Y, and tell me what else you have going on that can delay Y?" If the answers indicate a schedule risk, ask "How may I support you?" or "What can we defer or simplify?"

More work remains than can fit in remaining time, and the manager/ product owner tells the team "Do as much as you can" or "Try your best." These directives disempower the team: Would they *not* try their best without exhortation? Worse, they imply that being busy — and specifically, working individually and heads-down — is the road to success. An empowering, strategic alternative is to ask the team this: "Given our constraints and intended outcomes, what's the best way to move forward?" More specific follow-up questions are: "Which portions can we address later?" "What can we simplify?" "What can we renegotiate?"

Team member at a daily touchpoint: "I've worked on deliverable Z; my part is done." When you hear that, you know there are hand-offs and little teamwork. Instead, ask the team what they need to finish the entire deliverable.

Manager says to team member: "I need you to do task T. I know the team has already planned the next few days, but it shouldn't take more than a few hours." Beyond increasing workload, this interference (known as the "shoulder tap") invalidates both the team's planning mechanisms and their ability to commit to each other. Better to put task T in the queue of upcoming work (e.g., a backlog) and indicate its importance and urgency. If they are really higher than the team's other work, it will get done.

The organization is considering having the team work on a project, and the team's manager is asked: "What's your estimate for it?" or "When can you get started?" Since the manager isn't one of the workers, she shouldn't give a number and instead should ask *the team* for a *range*. Better yet, he or she should first help the stakeholders get clear on the intended *outcomes*, on how much achieving those outcomes is worth to them, and on the costs and consequences if they're delayed.

Director tells manager: "I need to take one of your people for a few weeks to help with project P." Instead of automatically saying, "Yes," the manager ought to discuss the consequences of this action to the team's productivity and well-being. In a world of "resources" who work on narrowly defined pieces, the consequence would be a simple reduction in output; in a world of human beings who build collaborative relationships and work toward shared outcomes, the consequence can be much worse. If the temporary reassignment is justified, the manager may still be transparent and empowering with the team by convening them, explaining the context and reasons, and then asking the team to choose who would go to that project. The alternative — deciding unilaterally, then being seen as yanking someone off the team — violates trust and safety, and conveys that "empowering" has been just talk.

Reflect and Improve Frequently

One choice you made when designing your workflow was the frequency of holding retrospectives: reflective team meetings designed for improvement of process and teamwork. Make sure each meeting has a facilitator, someone who will look after *the process of the meeting* but doesn't "own" it or preside over it. That person may be the team leader or even a team member, and may vary from one meeting to the next. When the team is still getting used to Agile, set aside 60-90 minutes for each retrospective — they'll need the time.

Expect most retrospectives to not have a set topic; instead, the participants will decide what to talk about. There are many good processes you can adopt and adapt;[7] here is the one I often use in the first few retrospectives with new Agile teams:

1. In the first five minutes, everyone writes down on sticky notes, one item per note, things of any significance that happened (or didn't but should have happened) since the last retrospective. This is factual recall, with neither interpretation nor judgment. When they are done, they post their stickies in no particular order on a wall, window, or whiteboard. Everybody reads everything, or the meeting leader reads them out loud, verbatim. They remove any duplicates and bring almost-duplicates or closely related notes together so as to make them look like a single big note. The point is to create a shared recollection of events without calling any of them out.

2. Every person, in silence, looks at each note and notices their personal reaction to it: very positive, positive, neutral, negative, very negative. They indicate any non-neutral reaction on the note or immediately beside it. (The team should agree on the legend for these indicators ahead of time; I usually provide green and red markers, and suggest using dots for low reactions and stars for heightened ones.)

3. The team now discusses the items that got the most pronounced reactions, whether positive or negative. Based on the texts, reactions, and any new thoughts, they draw insights and articulate learnings about successes, challenges, risks, gaps, and opportunities — anything that relates to their process and teamwork. The meeting facilitator captures their key points on a flipchart, whiteboard, or document. After 15-30 minutes, or when the list starts getting long, team members highlight the points they believe to have particular significance for them.

4. In the "now what?" stage, the team members look at the highlighted points and discuss what they'll do about them (or at least about the top few). The results of this conversation might be affirmation of what works, process changes, new or different working agreements, and experiments to try. Aim to have between one and three concrete, important changes or experiments, and ideally each should have a team member lead the charge on it.

In this process, it's the team's shared wisdom and interest that raise the topics most worthy of discussion, and it's the team that narrows down the topics and their responses to a manageable, focused set. Most of your retrospectives will be participant-driven like that. In addition, in the course of doing work, people might notice a topic that merits its own conversation. Three common early-day examples are: customers aren't providing meaningful early feedback; many work items languish in a "Blocked" state; we're not collaborating enough. For a topical retrospective, replace the first two steps in the process with the following:

1. On sticky notes, team members write their answers to predetermined, factual questions about the topic (for instance, "In the last few weeks, which kinds of items were blocked?" "What blocked each one?" "What did it take to release them?" For this particular topic, someone might collect relevant data ahead of the retrospective). Same de-duplication as above.

2. Every person, in silence, indicates on each note what kind of effect it had (positive, negative, neutral) on them or on the team. As above, agree on the legend or scale beforehand.

Breanna Ramos, HR Associate, TechSmith:

"We were used to frequent 'drive-by' interruptions, and assumed they were a noise we had no control over. After discussing this as a team, we're now tracking how disruptive they are and experimenting with solutions for gaining control."

The structural similarity between the attendee-generated and the topical retrospective agenda is not accidental. Both are based on the Focused Conversation Method, also known as ORID.[8] This four-part sequence starts with **O**bjective data, continues with **R**eflections on and **R**eactions to the data, proceeds to generate **I**nsights and **I**nterpretations of the data and the reflections, and closes with **D**ecisions for moving forward: recommendations, experiments, and action items. This powerful structure gives people room to think and collaborate, and prevents them from jumping to conclusions with partial information. (For an example of using ORID to solicit feedback on emerging deliverables, read endnote 9 of this chapter.) If you ever notice yourself approaching a retrospective as a free-form discussion, stop and consider following the ORID sequence instead.*

As the team discusses improvements to the process, help them be explicit about how those improvements implement the chosen values and principles — or not! Be careful with suggested changes "that worked for us in the past"; they might have been appropriate for pre-Agile ways of working and, as such, may be in conflict with what you're trying to achieve.

Similarly to treating the team's first Agile way of working as *experimental*, it helps to treat their process improvements as experimental. After all, even if the work is not complex, the team as a human system is. It's usually hard, or even impossible, to know how well some changes would work out. Moreover, since every change experience involves a chaos period (see "The Experience of Change" on page 53), treating each one as experimental makes them more palatable.

Retrospectives are terrific learning opportunities, both due to their structure and due to the mental pause from work. Make sure the team doesn't skip them. If you hear one of the following common reasons for skipping them, here is what you should do:

---

* A popular way to run retrospectives is to have everyone write down "what worked well" and "what could be improved," or "what to start/stop/change." This way is shorter, because it skips the O and the R steps of ORID. It's also less valuable for the same reason, as it effectively invites the team to offer solutions *before* they discuss problems.

✦ "We're too busy": allow them the time by factoring it into work plans.

✦ "Nothing ever changes as a result": help them act on their resolutions (the magic is in follow-up!).

✦ "We've made enough changes, and we're good now": help them see gaps between what they have and what they *could* have.

Ideally, reflection and improvement may happen after any activity and shouldn't have to wait for a recurring meeting. Realistically though, human beings seem to struggle with shifting quickly between doing and reflecting. Having scheduled opportunities helps make these mental shifts, but they can't be too far apart or people forget what their issues were or how they felt about them.

Lead Intentionally

Even before Agile came along, the word *leadership* had different semantics than *management*, although to this day many organizations continue to use the two interchangeably. The fundamental distinction is that you manage *things* but you lead *people* (the same person might do both). Agile favors *servant leadership*: the kind of leadership that creates conditions in which teams thrive and have the best chance of accomplishing their objectives. We touched on team-level leadership in chapter 8, and the expectation is for higher-level formal leaders to act that way as well.

Leadership is needed both for "regular" work and during times of change. Leadership creates culture, primarily through rewarding desirable behaviors and discouraging undesirable ones. Leadership is what separates engaged, responsible workforces from ones where people only check boxes on their job descriptions. As a leader, all your words and actions will affect the culture, whether you want them to or not; to affect it in a direction that will beget success, you must be *intentional*. Draw the mental picture, feel it in your bones, tell yourself the story of how you want your team and organization to be, and always lead toward that North Star. Culture change is usually slow and requires a lot of patience.[10]

Andy Plattner, Agile Coach, Daimler:

"Our Marketing team asked me, as the internal coach, for Agile training. In the next few weeks, they struggled with the process and the structure, but I wasn't available to help them beyond giving occasional feedback and recommendations. They tried following Scrum, but didn't appoint a Scrum Master of their own, nor did the team leader or manager step up to keep the change alive. The process slowly broke down and reverted to individual, specialized planning."

When it comes to creating an Agile culture, pay extra attention to the following matters:

SUPPORT PEOPLE THROUGH THE CHANGE. People are neither emotionless "resources" nor programmable units — change is personal and can be hard. A solid way to support them is to have frequent, regular one-on-ones with your team members. Every week or two, always at the same time, meet privately with a team member to talk about *them*. Focus on their growth, experiences, concerns, challenges, and suggestions. Use this time to mentor, coach, and listen; don't talk about work items or status — leave those matters to team settings. It's okay to point out problems and discuss solutions, but be sure to also acknowledge positives and appreciate efforts. As well, rely on the team's frequent touchpoints to serve as reminders that they are all in it together.

Nick Heling, Content Marketing Agile Coach, Red Hat:

"We are continuously reinventing our team structures to pragmatically meet our needs as we understand them in the moment. Our Scrum Masters help manage change fatigue and maintain continuity."

SUPPLEMENTARY RESOURCE: Download "How to Have One-on-One Meetings That Matter" from the book's companion website, **AgileForNonSoftwareTeams.com**.

START AND END WITH OUTCOMES. Whatever you discuss with the team, keep going back to its outcome/vision/objectives — why it matters — and help people see the meaning of their contribution.

DRAW AND DEFEND CLEAR BOUNDARIES. In an organization, nobody has 100% autonomy, which means there are always boundaries. Make sure your team is clear on their boundaries: What can they do and not do? What kinds of decisions are theirs to make? When should they work across boundaries? Boundaries of Agile teams tend to be wider than in controlled environments, but that width matters only if team members are aware of it.

WATCH THE WORK, NOT THE WORKERS. Your team deserves a work system that enables them to succeed. Continuously improve the system and develop the team, so that they can leverage their autonomy to consistently take responsible action.

REDUCE THE LOAD OF APPROVALS AND REVIEWS. Their inherent delays are one problem; when they signal mistrust of the workers, that can be a bigger problem. Get additional pairs of eyes on a deliverable when mistakes are likely or costly, or in regulatory compliance situations. Otherwise, consider different feedback loops that don't disempower people.

SET BEHAVIORAL EXPECTATIONS FOR PEOPLE. Specifically, expect them to demonstrate behaviors congruent with the chosen values and principles. Examples of such behaviors include explaining decisions (transparency), assuming positive intent on the part of others (respect), and seizing opportunities to work together rather than pass work to others (collaboration). Model these behaviors yourself, consistently and authentically.

LOOK TO THE SYSTEM, NOT THE PEOPLE, FOR EXPLANATIONS OF PROBLEM BEHAVIORS. When a team member exhibits a troubling or difficult behavior, your instinct might be to question their personality or motives. In many cases, their behavior is better explained by the system they're in; if you change the system, you'll get different behaviors.

> A highly competent and articulate team lead noticed that his director (who acted as the product owner) didn't appreciate his suggestions. To keep receiving his annual bonus, the team lead needed the director to give him a good annual review, so he learned to keep his mouth shut during retrospectives.
>
> At another company, a senior product owner was in charge of the project portfolio. I noticed that he wasn't spending any time prioritizing it, despite repeatedly agreeing with me about the importance of doing that. Later I learned that he simply didn't see the point, because almost every week the CEO would come in with ideas for new projects, and he had to stop the teams' current work and switch over to the new ones. In that management system, the portfolio didn't matter until the CEO changed his ways.

NOTICE HOW YOU COMMUNICATE AND ACT. Your pre-existing habits will reflect themselves in your behaviors and words, and some might negate your genuine attempts to lead people as suggested above. Self-awareness is *the* key for growth as an effective leader.

SEEK ALLIES AND SUPPORT. While one person can't change a work culture single-handedly, he or she *can* collaborate with enough other people to effect change. Rely on influential team members, peers, and executives throughout the journey. Reduce the magnitude and duration of the chaos stage by seeking customized assistance from Agile experts, whether internal or external.

Kerstin Bresler, Agile Coach:

"As a permanently employed coach and Scrum Master, I accompanied the Financial Control team for roughly half a year. I educated them on the Agile values and the Scrum framework, and helped them decide how to adjust the framework to their context. Later the team and the manager told me that they wouldn't have done it as intensively as they did if I hadn't been available to them."

I can't do proper justice to the matter of Agile leadership in this brief space. For a much deeper dive into it, read my book *The Human Side of Agile*. It's organized as answers to the most pressing questions Agile leaders have.

Assess How It's Going

Whether you treat your new way of working as an experiment or as a certainty, you'd do well to frequently assess how it's going. Doing that will allow you to identify the areas most deserving of recognition or in most need of help. There are two parts to this assessment.

1. How Well Are You Following the Principles You've Chosen?

You started designing your new way of working by choosing operating principles. Then you designed tactics, such as roles, practices, and touchpoints based on those principles. Now, evaluate what's *actually* happening: for each principle on your list, score how well your *current* tactics implement it. You might do this yourself, or ask each team member to do this scoring from their own perspective, then tabulate the results and examine them. I like to use a 1-5 scale, where 1, 3, and 5 are defined as follows, and 2 and 4 are intermediary points:

✦ 1 (low): we apply this principle partially and inconsistently

✦ 3 (medium): we're mostly doing it, but it requires constant intention and attention

✦ 5 (high): this principle is now ingrained in everything we do; it feels like second nature

If you have more than one team, assess each one separately, based on their own principles. If the teams are closely related and are trying to exhibit a similar mind-set, also note the consistency of each principle's application (the spread of its distribution) across the teams.

Keeping with my general theme of "do what you think is right for you," notice how this assessment works. You're not checking *compliance* with a framework's or someone's checklist of roles, practices, artifacts, and meetings. Nor are you looking for evidence of "Agile behaviors" if your chosen way of working isn't fully Agile in the first place. Instead, you're assessing *congruence* between what you intended to do, based on values and beliefs, and the behaviors you actually see; you're examining how *systematically* you're applying your principles in the experiment. I'll say it again: your way of working doesn't have to look like anyone else's.

Conducting this informal, imprecise assessment should take you or the team no more than 30 minutes. Do it every few weeks and discuss the results with them in a safe space. You should see improvement over time, but don't expect it to be smooth. When the numbers are generally 1 or 2, it's an indication that you're actively trying to create a new way of working, but it's not distinct enough (or hasn't taken hold) yet. Together with the team, try to understand whether that's simply the Satir model's chaos stage, or whether they're not going further because their attempts so far have actually produced adverse results.

The numbers must stabilize at 3 or higher for you to say that the team truly has a new way of working. It will probably be months before this happens! When it does, you can move to the more important questions:

2. How, and How Much, Is Your Team More Successful Now? What Sort of Downsides Accompany that Success?

Answering these questions will tell you whether the mind-set you've espoused, and are manifesting in your tactics, does in fact get the results you hoped for when you began this journey. Be aware, though, that some business outcomes are extremely hard to measure, and some changes in them will be unrelated to your new way of working. Therefore, at this point, a qualitative or subjective assessment will serve you better than hard-and-fast metrics (chapter 10 dives deeper into many reasons for this statement). However you approach it, you must be able to gather some convincing evidence to justify continuing the experiment.

Trying a new way of working is hard. Trying an Agile one, with its complexity and discipline, takes extra patience and resilience. So celebrate progress frequently, and use setbacks as learning opportunities. It will be several months before you can say, "We've got the hang of Agile." This will be your evidence:

+ You're now completing meaningful deliverables at a more-even rate and with less stress than before.

+ Your customers and stakeholders like what they're getting, and it's helping them accomplish their outcomes better.

+ The team is really working as a team.

+ The process has become easy for the team, and they can explain how every part of it manifests their desired values.

Once you're there, turn to chapter 10 for guidance on expanding and increasing Agility.

SUPPLEMENTARY RESOURCES

Go to **AgileForNonSoftwareTeams.com** and download
"Collaboration Etiquette Posters" and
"How to Have One-on-One Meetings That Matter."

Chapter 10
Increase and Expand Agility

Even if your experiment has covered only one kind of work, that's an achievement! If you and the team haven't celebrated progress so far, now is the time to do so. As well, consider running a two- to three-hour retrospective to generate high-level insights and learnings about the journey so far. This is the earliest point to consider making permanent some of the experiment's aspects, such as the roles or seating arrangement. And when you're ready to expand and increase agility, this chapter will give you ideas. We start with increasing the agility of your current Agile implementation, continue with expanding its scope, and close with pitfalls to watch out for.

Continuous Improvement

The Agile mind-set is emphatic about *continuous improvement:* teams should regularly and collaboratively improve their product and way of working within the context of their values and beliefs. The assumption is that, being closest to their work, teams should know what to improve, figure out how to do that, and own the actions. While this is an empowering perspective, teams sometimes feel stuck or unsure how to proceed. Here are a number of ideas that many people have found useful.

SIMPLIFY. While some of your work is likely complex, not all complexity is born equal. Some is *essential:* it is due to the nature of the work. The rest of it is *accidental:* the team causes it by the way they work.[1] For example, the task of assembling a 2,000-piece jigsaw puzzle has a high level of essential complexity, determined by the puzzle's picture and the shapes of the pieces. If I try to assemble the puzzle on a small table that already has other things on it (coffee mugs, headphones, books), I'm causing accidental complexity that will make my work harder. There's usually little you can do about essential complexity (other than, most likely, letting technology handle it). Instead, look for accidental complexity, understand its causes, and strive to reduce it.

ELIMINATE WASTE. Waste, a term from Lean thinking,[2] refers to anything in the workflow that doesn't add value to the deliverable. Non-Agile, non-Lean processes are often riddled with waste, which gives rise to a powerful insight: you might increase productivity and throughput more by eliminating some of the wasteful parts of the workflow (which is relatively easy to do) than by improving the productive parts (which can be quite hard to do, and they may already be quite efficient). Here are the seven categories of waste, along with some common examples:

1. Overproduction: rarely used or just-in-case deliverables; "bells and whistles"; solutions to more or bigger problems than necessary

2. Partially done work: collecting requirements, creating designs, or writing drafts that never make it to a deliverable; producing deliverables that don't get approved

3. Relearning: going back to forgotten subject matter or procedures; reacquiring knowledge; revisiting/updating requirements and plans; checking something more than once

4. Hand-offs: moving work between team members, incurring delays and losing information along the way

5. Task switching: working on two or more deliverables in parallel; interrupting focused work for meetings, questions, or incidents

6. Delays: waiting for someone who has necessary information or other inputs; waiting for approval

7. Defects: problems found in work that was done earlier; problems that recur because the first fix wasn't good; collecting, managing, and prioritizing defects to fix

As you were reading each waste category, did you think "Yep, we've got that one!"? Then you're in good company. Nobody ever gets to 0% waste, but considering the typical starting point, any reduction is welcome. The Agile principles explained in this book go a long way toward reducing waste. For instance, collaborating with the customer on what's really needed reduces overproduction, and finishing started items (instead of starting many ones) reduces partially done work. Look at your workflow, identify the waste you have at each point, and focus on the worst offenders. You might decide not to invest in reducing some of them; for the others, consider changes to the workflow, policies, or team structure that may reduce the waste, hopefully with minimal side effects.

TIGHTEN THE WORKFLOW. When you designed the workflow in chapter 8, my advice was to keep it simple; the goal was to get started easily with something workable. In chapter 9, the advice was to limit WIP on intermediate workflow stages, clear congestion, manage blockers, and codify your response to emergencies; the goal was to stabilize the system and settle on a sustainable pace. Two additional actions you can take now for better flow are:

+ Assess the board's fit for purpose. As a visual representation of the work's state and flow, how well does it help everyone see and manage the flow? Get with the team and ask yourselves:

  ⬦ How does the board help us implement our work principles? (For example, does it help us pick the most important work to do? Does its physical layout help us constrain our workload?)

  ⬦ How does the board make it hard for us to follow our principles? (For instance, do its columns imply that people should focus on their individual "parts" instead of on the whole? Does the board encourage people to just move work along instead of bringing it to the high standard we defined for "done"?)

  ⬦ Does anyone do work that's never reflected on the board? (For example, are people finding it necessary to make their own personal work lists? Do they get assigned additional tasks, which compromise their availability to this team?)

  ⬦ Are the columns (work states) useful? (If they are too general or high-level, it's hard to know what goes on with a task; if they are too specific, managing the board can become a headache.)

Chris Taylor, CEO, Fisher's Tech:

"Our main board represented new work, but we didn't have a good handle on the flow of problem-solving. So we added a board near the main one; employees are surfacing problems all the time and posting them in the leftmost column. Management meets every week to prioritize them and choose problems for the week, and each item receives someone's commitment to getting it solved. A problem moves to 'Done' (the rightmost column) if the right people got together, understood the root cause, and produced an action plan. In addition to actually solving our problems, this board communicates to everyone that problems get taken care of."

+ Set explicit policies around items entering the workflow, moving through its stages, and coming out of it. Say, for example, that a single person manages and sequences most work items, but other people sometimes add their own items to the front of the queue (this is a very common situation for early-stage teams). In this case, you'd get the team together and determine or improve the policy for putting *any* item in the queue; that will increase consistency and transparency, and allow everyone to act more strategically. In other examples, you might define a policy for dealing with items that sit too long in some mid-workflow state, or policies for handling routine and minor ad-hoc tasks.

Kerstin Bresler, Agile Coach:

"The Financial Control team and their manager were frustrated about not being able to get their planned work done. After collecting stats over a couple of iterations, they were shocked to realize that 40% of their work was *unplanned*. They found that all unplanned and short-notice requests came from upper management, including their second-level manager — the same people who were also expecting planned work to get done within original time frames. After a simple conversation with management, they upgraded their process, and were able to reduce unplanned work to 15% on average. Moving forward, they left a 15% buffer in each iteration for unplanned work; anytime the need was less, they pulled in other tasks from the prioritized backlog."

MAKE OPPORTUNITIES FOR LEARNING. The more people learn — about the work, each other, their technology, their customers — the better their results. The good teamwork and feedback loops you've established will be a great start toward amplifying the team's learning, and there's room for a lot more. Spend time observing your customers at work, experiment, reflect after activities, teach each other skills, hold study groups and book clubs, get ideas from other people in the organization who are also trying on new ways of working. Be aware, though, all these ideas require some *slack*: a bit of time, intentionally allocated to rest, learning, or defocusing and *not* to mission-critical work or other busyness.[3]

UPGRADE THE TEAM SPACE. If your team has got this far without colocating, and colocation is a viable option, now might be a good time to float the idea without encountering too much resistance. And if they are already colocated, consider experimenting with the design of their space because every *detail matters*. Distances between team members, who sits next to whom, visual and auditory distractions, foot traffic, what's on the walls — these aspects often have outsized effects on communication, collaboration, and focus, and therefore on results. Make sure the team is consistently involved in the design of their space.

KEEP ASKING, "HOW DO WE KNOW?" People like to think they're right, and in your interactions with team members, managers, and stakeholders, they will probably sound rather confident. Confidence blinds people to their risk of being wrong. An Agile mind-set, intent on doing more of the right and less of the wrong, requires a certain level of humility.[4] Develop the habit, in yourself and in your team, of checking your assumptions and validating your choices, by asking questions like these: How we do know that we're prioritizing work effectively? That we understand a business problem correctly? That our intended solution is viable? That the solution we've developed is correct? That the feedback we've solicited is honest? The more you leave to confidence and assumptions, the more luck you'll need to succeed.

Expanding the Scope of Agility

With the experiment a success, you might wish to apply Agile to more or bigger undertakings. Each kind of expansion has its own challenges and options.

Same Team, More Kinds of Work

In chapter 4, you made an inventory of your work, and chose a subset of that work for the Agile experiment. The team may now be ready to expand their new approach to address another item from that list. Perhaps that's a different product, service, or solution; perhaps it's some other major responsibility or activity. Repeat the rest of the guidance in chapter 4, and if Agile is suitable for the new choice, repeat chapter 8. It will be much easier and quicker this time.

With the team tackling two or more different kinds of work using Agile concepts, you will now need to make an additional decision: how to keep work management easy. You might want to have separate workflows and separate boards; if you do, try to locate them side by side. Another common solution is to capture everything on a single board; you might dedicate a swim lane (horizontal portion of the board) to each kind of work, or color-code items based on their area. The principle behind these solutions is to see and manage everything in one place, so the team can apportion their efforts effectively.

More of the Value Stream

Another way to increase agility is by extending the scope of the team's responsibility, and likely also their membership, to include more of the "value stream." This concept refers to the entire flow of work, starting from a customer order or an approved initiative and ending in the customer's and business's realizing some benefit.

For example, say you manage a large bookstore, and you've implemented Agile principles at the checkout. The staff there work as a team now, focus on the outcome of patron satisfaction with the checkout experience, and arrange their shifts themselves. The checkout is part of a larger value stream, which starts with a person walking in looking for interesting books, and ends when the person has found some and paid for them. Implementing agility to the buyer's journey might improve customer outcomes, such as satisfaction, and business outcomes, such as revenue per visit. In general, allowing teams responsibility over entire value streams tends to be a great way to build a "one team" culture of engagement and contribution while reducing the perceived need to ensure accountability.

Carry out this type of extension by repeating the guidance of chapters 4 and 8. While workflow design will be familiar, you may well have to increase the size of the team and involve people from diverse functions and specialties. Usually, this requires people to pitch in in more areas. Some will appreciate the opportunity to contribute and to grow, and some won't, especially if they self-identify with their role or think they're above the pay grade of a specific responsibility. As before, imposing Agile on them is a nonstarter; opt for invitation, and remind them this is still an experiment. Whether it succeeds or fails, all of you will emerge from it knowing more about your choices and preferences.

More Teams, Doing Different Work

You've experimented with Agile for one team, and now another team is interested. If the two teams rarely depend on each other for completing work, that's easy: follow the guidance of the previous chapters and get them started. They might end up designing a similar process, or not. Don't try to standardize their process or copy-paste what the first team used; they are different people in a different context, and they deserve a way of working that fits their situation. However, encourage them to frequently look for opportunities to learn from each other.

More Teams, Doing Codependent Work

Having figured out Agile for one team, you might wish to try it on work that requires two or more teams. In project management terms, this would be a *program*: the teams produce related deliverables, which form part of a bigger whole, and the whole isn't viable without all the parts. For example, a car comprises many separately produced parts, which are all required for the car to be usable and commercially viable, such as engine, doors, mirrors, transmission, and tires.

When managing a program in an Agile way, implement the same principles you'd have chosen for the single team. After all, the importance of matters such as outcome orientation, frequent feedback, and cost of change minimization has nothing to do with staff size. However, expect the process to require more effort and time than in the single-team case (though not necessarily more so than your pre-Agile methods). Usually, the biggest challenge is the decision-making, coordination, and communication needed to keep people working toward the same outcomes. Hence, solutions commonly include program-level boards and meetings in addition to team-level ones, plus more reliance on managers' support for impediment removal and schedule coordination. The biggest pitfall seems to be a bounce-back to the previous value and belief system; for instance, relying on centralized, top-down planning, or each team caring only about doing their isolated "part."

In the more challenging case, the program teams also have technical dependencies on each other. Not only do their deliverables need to make coherent sense together, what goes into those deliverables involves and affects multiple teams. For example, corporate branding requires consistency of messaging and design across the company's products, physical presence, and communication channels, all of which are likely the responsibility of different teams. This situation is called "Agile at scale." Of particular concern is the cost of change, which can grow rapidly if people make local choices that have global effect. In a scaling situation, more people need to expend more energy on decision-making, coordination, and communication. On a technical level, they must continuously connect ("integrate") the small work done by different teams in order to surface dependencies and prevent nasty surprises early. The closer these people are to the level where real work gets done, the faster and better those decisions are likely to be made. A related helpful pattern is to allow people freedom to move among the program's teams as work needs warrant.

This brings us to the matter of moving people around, which becomes a popular option when work spans a long time or many people. In many large organizations that are used to the matrix structure, this option is also the reality, and teams disband after their projects end. The Agile community, by contrast, has been quite vocal about keeping teams stable, so they can build the relationships and collaborative work habits that enable high performance. Rather than shift "resources" (who are human beings!) based on the work, the idea is to have stable teams consistently take in ("pull") the most important work. While theoretically sound and in line with the Agile principles, in your context this approach may bump into availability, skill, and motivation challenges. You have a strategic choice to make here; be careful not to default to traditional "resource planning" merely because it's familiar and commonplace. In many conditions, the performance of stable, solid, collaborative teams far outweighs the sum of individuals' performance.[5]

When the overall group is not so large that some people don't know others, there is a middle ground.

Nick Heling, Content Marketing Agile Coach, Red Hat:

"We've created a subteam within our larger Scrum team. The subteam works separately from the primary team, focusing on achieving results related to a specific key performance indicator (KPI) that our Chief Marketing Officer identified as a goal for this year. They have their own product owner, a well-defined and frequently prioritized backlog of work, and a workflow based on sprints with WIP limits. Members from the primary team cycle into this subteam for a period of two or three sprints. We're finding that the change in focus and workflow has been boosting team morale by providing novelty and a change of pace."

Metrics and Measurements

Chapter 9 provided a few simple questions to check that the team was indeed working in a new way that was worth keeping. At this point, you (or your management) might be looking for additional metrics and measures.

The subject of metrics is immense, and continues to spark raging debates within the Agile community. It is also the subject of uncomfortable arguments between Agile coaches and executives, especially when the latter believe "You can't manage what you can't measure." (Many Agilists, who don't agree with this belief, will nonetheless agree with "You can't manage what you can't *see*.") In more than 20 years of struggling with this matter in the context of software development, the Agile community has come to several realizations, as described below.[6] You may not agree with all of them, but do give them serious thought as you choose metrics for your work context.

While it's easy to come up with metrics, it's very difficult to come up with **metrics that matter**.[7] To give a personal example, I follow my books' sales reports. Low numbers discourage me, and what's worse, I can't know why they're low. If the numbers are high, I feel great that people like my work, although I don't have data for how many buyers actually *read* and then benefit from the books. Similarly, it is relatively easy to measure local improvements or changes, but harder to correlate them to system-wide effects that are of greater interest to the business.

A common pitfall, when good metrics are hard to collect, is to **read too much** into easier metrics. For example, a popular measure of Scrum team performance is velocity: how many units of effort (called "points") they complete in an average iteration/sprint. It is a reasonable measure of capacity, often useful for planning purposes, and easy to calculate. Many people also use it as an indicator of performance, without gathering further evidence that the team's capacity goes toward impactful, finished work. (That is merely *assumed*, because Scrum teams generally work in priority sequence and have a definition of "done.") It's akin to measuring economical value creation by calculating the gross domestic product, which also captures a lot of necessary but non-value-adding work such as snow removal, waste management, and road maintenance.

Turning to **traditional process metrics** for ideas doesn't always help in an Agile setting. Usually, that's because they reflect activities or artifacts, but not impact. For example, assessing my progress on this book by counting the hours, words, or sections I write every day won't help me know whether I'm using my time effectively. Only if the numbers are very low will I know something useful: that I'm not making much progress.

Since it's human beings who analyze metrics, a host of **cognitive biases** affect their interpretation. For instance, if I told you, "My team gets a velocity of 8 points per sprint," would you consider that good? If I had said instead, "They get 24 points per sprint," would you have been more impressed? A team that wants to make a good impression only needs to change the size of a point, as governments used to do with their currencies. Or say the team's velocity is consistent for four sprints, and in the fifth it drops by 25%. That drop might invite scrutiny and uncomfortable conversations with management, even though it could also be due to natural variation in the system.

Which brings us to the matter of management attention. Metrics don't only assess a system of interest; they **influence people's behavior**, for better or worse. Of course, management's intent is usually to influence behavior for the better, but their metrics sometimes adversely affect other desirable behaviors.[8] They do so by creating artificial competition ("salesperson of the month!"), by triggering limited-supply incentives ("close more sales, get a bonus!"), or by compromising psychological safety ("you're not closing enough sales!"). To make matters worse, some metrics might imply there's a problem with a team, when the root cause is the system they work in.

John Hill, Agile Coach and Trainer:

"Several years ago I had an Agile transformation client that awarded an individual the monthly 'Game Changer' designation, accompanied by a trophy and gift card. Virtually every time this reward was presented, I could see the body language of the other members of that team and feel their resentment for not being appreciated for their contributions as part of the same team."

When discussing metrics with management, the focus will likely be work-related: how much, how fast, how well. Since Agile is fiercely people-first, be sure to also pay attention to **people's engagement** and to factors that affect it. You might measure individual engagement,[9] team health,[10] motivation, or morale. Recall the fundamental Agile worldview introduced in chapter 1: healthy teams that consistently delight customers will achieve great business results. If you truly agree with it, ensuring that your teams are healthy and fully customer-minded may considerably reduce the emphasis you place on assessing their work methods.

Warning, Dangers Ahead

No case of organizational change is without its pitfalls and dangers. Even once you're truly Agile, what can derail further improvements and the spread of Agility, or even cause a reversal?

The Lure of Standards, Frameworks, and "Best Practices"

If you've followed my guidance in this book, your way of working fits your needs. Its tactics — practices, roles, artifacts, meetings, and so on — are your creation. I hope your team feels that they own their methods, and can adapt them as necessary.

And yet, throughout this journey, I bet you've heard some of the following questions, or wondered about them yourself:

+ "What's the best way to...?"

+ "What's the right way to...?"

+ "All our other teams do [daily standup/user stories/sprint demos, etc.]; shouldn't we do those as well?"

+ "Are we following Agile best practices?"

+ "Are we doing this right?"

Why am I sure about that? Because at least one third of a typical population prefers to follow proven procedures,[11] and many procedures have been documented and billed as proven or "best practices." Many of those appear in books and blogs, and are taught in courses that carry the extra cachet of certification. For these reasons, you'll hear about many teams using them, which may reinforce their perception as valuable, necessary, or best. Yet that doesn't make them best *for you*. For every known Agile practice, I can give you examples of teams that didn't find it helpful or workable. Don't take them on because of a halo effect.

While there is no Agile standard, there are plenty of good ideas out there, which you might find useful, intriguing, or an inspiration for better tactics or principles for your team. Strip the words "best," "standard," and "right" from them, and consider them promising ideas that have worked for some people.

The risk, however, is not only from outside; you might be under pressure from above to force-fit your process into some organizational standard. This is bad news; while it makes large-scale management easier, it compromises safety and agency, and reduces the potential success of individual teams. Instead, help your management establish a coherent culture around explicit values, beliefs, and behaviors within which semiautonomous teams choose how they work.

Cultural Pull and Drift

The organizational culture needs to be ready, willing, and able to adopt Agile for it to stick and eventually become the norm. That means having a sufficient level of people-orientation, empowerment, psychological safety, tolerance of ambiguity, and openness, among other things. In turn, intentional Agility reinforces such a culture. You can't really have one without the other.

Cultures, however, are not static. Influential or powerful individuals change cultures intentionally through their words and actions. People also change cultures unintentionally, which I think of as drift. Drift is slow, gradual, and rarely noticed. For instance, organizations don't start out rife with blaming and cynicism, but can get this way through many instances of opaque and siloed decision-making.

Rebecca Jensen, CEO, Midwest Real Estate Data (MRED):

"When I came on board as the CEO four years ago, the office culture was overly formal and based on the enforcement of strict rules that limited the development of relationships. All offices were located on this long corridor, and everyone worked behind closed doors. There was little trust between departments: even the copy machine was locked down. It got to be this way over a long period of time. Before we even tried Agile, we modernized the space, created common areas, and moved offices so that teams were near each other and could collaborate more easily. We restructured some jobs, introduced the concept of people backing each other up, and I had to let some people go. A rebranding effort last year also helped reinforce our new culture. We also hire differently now: the team recommends a candidate to hire, and I only meet that person toward the end of the hiring process."

You can, and should, have a positive pull on the culture by being intentional and explicit about the substance of your leadership. Monitor changes at the top that may derail your efforts, and pay attention to cultural drift. If you notice any, reversing it should be a priority for you.

David Johnson, company name withheld:

"18 months into a successful transformation and new product development, the visionary leaders departed for other ventures. The company loved the new product, our customers got super excited, and capital flowed in. Lots of new folks were hired to try to enhance throughput. We were cutting corners, with half the product teams failing to apply basic principles. Schedules got tight and feature scheduling got out of whack. Micromanagement and mistrust started to reach critical mass and fostered such poor working conditions that many key subject matter and technical experts have moved on. Now we have many replacements, even more process, lower throughput, less data-driven decision-making, and more whim."

Managing People

Much accepted wisdom and common sense around engaging, culti-vating, and retaining people actually diminishes agility.

One such organizational staple is performance management. In its traditional form, which takes the industrial perspective that people are "resources" to be utilized, managers use appraisals, threats, and incen-tives to "fix" people. In an Agile environment, which invites and allows agency and teamwork, this mechanism reduces agency and drives wedges between team members. To the extent you can, replace formal evaluations with frequent coaching based on observations, empathy, and honest feedback.

Another organizational standby is accountability, meaning the per-formance of assigned tasks per expectations and the ability to render an account of shortfalls. That, as in the case of performance man-agement, is not a perspective of agency or willing behavior. "Holding people accountable" makes the hidden assumption that without it, their actions would fall short of requirements or standards. An Agile mind-set prefers trust to accountability, believing that treating people as responsible adults and making it possible for them to succeed will yield higher engagement and better results. Throughout your Agile journey, you'll see instances of accountability instead of trust; strive to change that conversation.

The third matter has to do with motivating people. Three kinds of motivators exist:

✦ Intrinsic motivators come from within the person. These include autonomy (the ability to make important decisions), mastery (getting good at something important to the person), purpose (doing work that matters to them), enjoyability (of the work), and challenge.[12]

✦ Extrinsic motivators come from outside. These include rewards (promotions, bonuses, gift cards), recognition (non-monetary acknowledgment, feedback, thanks), and praise (which is recognition with judgment, as in "Great job! You're an A player!").

✦ Hygiene factors are elements whose absence demotivates people. Examples include acceptable working conditions, a salary they can live on, a competent manager, a psychologically safe environment, and knowing how to succeed.

Considerable field research and empirical evidence have shown that while rewards and praise — which are ubiquitous in the workplace — can alter behaviors short-term, they have little staying power. And long-term, they may reduce motivation as people start caring more about the rewards than the work. When applied to individuals instead of teams, they also create subtle (or not so subtle) competition. On the other hand, intrinsic motivators — which are individual and can't be standardized — have a stronger staying power and give rise to a healthier culture that aligns with the Agile ideals. As a leader, provide the hygiene factors and maintain the conditions that keep your team intrinsically motivated. Recognize team and individual contributions, because people do want to feel important and for their work to be noticed, but dial back on rewards and praise.

Rebecca Jensen:

"We have cross-functional teams work on strategic initiatives, so we don't do individual bonuses anymore. Instead, a percentage of revenue goes into a bonus pool, and each initiative is allocated a percentage of the bonus pool. If it's completed, 50% of the initiative's share is paid equally among all staff and the other 50% is proportional to each staff member's salary."

In chapter 5, I said that an Agile transformation is arguably the deepest form of organizational change a person will experience in his or her career. And as you have seen in the chapters since then, doing it properly is a great deal of work. There is much to notice, to do, to not do, to communicate, to explain. Helping people succeed with Agile has been my life's work — and I wouldn't trade it for anything. I wish you the same experience.

Epilogue
A Glimpse into the Future

Perhaps you picked up this book because your company is pursuing an Agile transformation; many do these days. And if the initiative has been your own, your successes (and those of colleagues or competitors) might trigger an executive interest in organizational agility. Today's fast-changing, customer-oriented business landscape makes it less and less optional.

Organizational agility has many definitions. One is the ability to build the right things, build them right, and build at the right speed, optimizing for organizational flow.[1] Another one is being adaptive, creative, and resilient when dealing with complexity, uncertainty, and change.[2] However it's defined, and despite differences in tactics, Agile organizations have a great deal in common in terms of the values, principles, and habits I've described in this book. If that's your future, years away, what might it be like? Here is a glimpse.

In an Agile organization, more people face the customers, act entrepreneurially, and determine direction. Even with a titular hierarchy, the company is actually organized as a network of teams; roles are decoupled from titles, and people may choose their teams. Everything teams do is oriented toward product, service, solution, outcome, and value, though they might still treat some of their work as projects. While organized along value streams, folks associate with same-role colleagues for career development, mutual learning, and consistency.

As groups evolve, they become less siloed and align more to other groups in their pursuit of bigger outcomes. In increasingly more cases, where a group would have otherwise treated another one as a customer, the two groups would act as partners, with staff collaborating directly without waiting for approval, permission, or task assignment. Moreover, they reshape their deliverables in support of greater organizational agility; for example, Finance generally moves away from predictive, annual, project-based budgeting to value-stream and team-based funding.

Managers in an Agile organization, which is flatter than is currently the norm, are enablers of decisions made by people closer to the work. Managers associate themselves with teams, value streams, and capabilities rather than with narrow functions. Teams of managers form and reform to manage the work portfolio, support initiatives, learn together, and improve the system iteratively. They invest considerable time coaching current and up-and-coming leaders, which further enables distributed decision-making and Agility.

Chris Taylor, CEO, Fisher's Tech:

"Our master board, visible to everyone in headquarters, reflects our backlog of projects. It is prioritized along two axes: increasing profitability and increasing customer happiness. Our senior team (all VPs) have a weekly standup in front of it to review progress and make new choices. Every quarter, we review how our choices turned out and learn from that."

One of the responsibilities of leaders is to be intentional about the culture they want. Initially, the motivation and focus are on improving the organization's ways of working for better business outcomes. Later, the organization shifts from being a brand that's Agile to being an Agile brand.

Rebecca Jensen, CEO, Midwest Real Estate Data (MRED):

"We count over 45,000 real estate professionals among our customers. We've learned that they like working iteratively and being involved. They are feeling the love: they know we're customer-driven and that the feedback they give us doesn't go into a black hole. In four years, our Net Promoter Score went from 44 to 65!"

In 2001, a group of thought leaders penned the *Manifesto for Agile Software Development*, which they opened with these words: "We are uncovering better ways of developing software by doing it and helping others do it." In the 18 years since then, humanity continues to uncover better ways to do *all kinds of work*, and the quest is not over. Where will we go next?

STORIES FROM THE FIELD

This appendix contains stories from diverse non-software Agile implementations. My goals in choosing these specific accounts have been to demonstrate that Agile is being used successfully in diverse business settings (some of them may even be like yours), to expand your thinking in terms of potential ways to apply the Agile mind-set, and to further impress upon you that getting there takes effort, time, and support.

Marketing Team at a Technology Company
(Contributed by Kerstin Bresler, Agile Coach)

The team consisted of 15 people at the company's headquarters in Germany, and 2-3 in each of the company's subsidiaries in San Francisco and Singapore. They designed, built, and maintained the company's Internet presence, managed its social media channels, and created promotional material. Every year, they worked on several time-constrained projects: organizing customer-focused events and exhibiting the company's products at trade shows. In addition, the team regularly had to act on short-notice, high-urgency requests from the CEO. The team looked for methods for handling all types of work effectively. In particular, those methods should create good transparency, facilitate communication and collaboration, and support prioritization with their stakeholders. As the Agile coach on staff, I supported them during the first year of their Agile journey.

We started with the headquarters team, which had the majority of people and workload; we planned to keep the other locations' staff up to date via already-established weekly calls. During a half-day workshop they defined an initial workflow, decided how to display it on a whiteboard, chose the information to capture on tasks' sticky notes, and determined policies for task management. Within the first four weeks they revised the workflow twice, adding steps as they realized the need for them. After that, they switched to an electronic tool, which enabled sharing and transparency for anyone across all regions. The team played around with various visualizations. For example, they created swim lanes to represent task areas, and tried color-coding for priorities and due dates.

In their second week, the team started reflecting regularly on the process and adjusting it every time they detected something. For example, they learned that assigning tasks and adding task comments in the electronic tool, despite triggering notifications to the task assignee, was no replacement for personal, verbal communication. They also realized that the daily standups — held first in front of the whiteboard, and later in front of a monitor displaying the electronic task board — were just long and boring status updates. It took them several weeks to upgrade the daily meeting to a team conversation. And while the task board kept reflecting the entire workload, the team continued to manage the specifics of event planning with a traditional project plan, whose visualization of dates and dependencies made scheduling tasks easier.

The team took almost half a year to turn their various practices and policies into *habits*. When I left them, a year after they started, they felt good about their progress. The electronic task board represented all the work, including external dependencies; for instance, it now had a column for "this task is currently in progress outside the team." They were conducting daily standups in each location, and providing summaries to the other locations on a chat channel. Workload balancing improved, and they noticed and responded to stuck tasks sooner. They held a retrospective in each location every six weeks, and an all-hands retrospective twice a year (on-site or with a remote collaboration tool). They were not able to influence the CEO to change his habit of bringing them short-notice work and wanting his tasks done first. However, the task board helped the team negotiate better timelines, especially when working on his tasks conflicted with time-constrained trade show planning, and gave visibility to stakeholders whose deliverables it delayed.

Office Design and Build-out
(Contributed by Arjay Hinek, Agile Continuous Improvement Coach, Red Hat)

The company has been expanding rapidly — now at over 16,000 employees worldwide — and an ongoing concern is where to put them all. As the company has a strong focus on a common culture, the two prime directives for every new or refurbished office are: (1) every employee's connectivity experience should be the same across the world, and (2) every office should reflect the city in which it is located. For a long time, however, the two groups that make it happen — Office Design and Technical Delivery — were not in sync. There was no sense of partnership around a shared vision due to poor communication and coordination.

The leadership from both groups decided to try applying Agile principles in an effort to improve communication on an upcoming high-profile project. They invited me to help. I felt the keys were to ensure that everyone had real visibility into what each group needed at a high level, and to get them to agree on an evolutionary path for the project (its "spine"). Working with the teams (not only their managers), we conducted a decentralized planning workshop modeled after story mapping[1] focusing on the very sequential activities of building a new office. It wasn't a smooth or pretty process, but they started spotting ill-timed dependencies on things as simple as furniture ordering and intended room use. Equally valuable was the shared mental model they developed for the project. It was a first, and it created a true "team."

We started with Scrum on the project, but struggled to make it work. Over time, the teams honed their way of working, now called "Pragmatic Delivery," based on five practices that they performed with an Agile mind-set:

1. Decentralized planning (mapping) at the beginning of a project

2. Team standards, owned and developed by the team

3. Twice-a-week standup meetings

4. Increased visibility using rolling, look-ahead planning

5. Frequent retrospectives

We did have some hiccups along the way. For instance, the teams tried to use the Agile planning tools that Red Hat's software engineers favored, but found them uncomfortable and went back to Excel. We also realized that not all team members had their voices heard in the creation of this way of working. On the other hand, we saw improvement in unexpected places. For example, one of the project managers started using daily standups with his trades vendors; he had greater visibility into their progress, and they had a much clearer idea of when their work would be needed.

The most significant development, however, was a policy that leadership established: any external project management group had to agree to include those five baseline practices in their methodology before a contract could be signed.

Biotech R&D

(Contributed by Camilla Frederikke Clauson-Kaas, Troels Vincents Hjortholm, and Terkel Tolstrup, Agile Coaches with Deloitte Consulting Denmark; written three months into the Agile journey)

The company operates in the biotech industry, competing in a global market where innovation and speed in new product development are of the essence. Intrigued by IT's use of Agile to prove impact quickly and continuously, project and senior managers from the molecular formulation R&D department decided to try Agile on their new development program. They chose a pilot project, consisting of four teams of chemists and lab technicians distributed across three countries, and focused on developing new molecular formulations to support consumer products.

With our facilitation, the project and senior management team initiated the journey by implementing the following: two-week sprints with colocation timeslots, planning events, review meetings, minimum viable product (MVP) planning, retrospective events, and backlog refinement meetings. Initially, a commercial representative as well as senior management acted as business owners to set direction and continuous prioritization, and the project manager acted as product owner.

The beginning was rough. Already after the first planning event, the teams were impatient, saying Agile was too chaotic and didn't work for them. These reactions remained during the sprint and through its closing retrospective, even though both actually went well from an Agile standpoint. We, the coaches, felt we hadn't prepared the teams and management enough; we had to make an effort to help the teams understand the process and the effort it takes to establish a completely new way of planning their work. Nevertheless, they agreed to continue with the Agile experiment for at least two or three months before deciding whether Agile ways of working would actually work well in this setting.

A bit into the process, it became clear that senior management expected Agile to be a quick fix for lack of motivation. This did not happen. While sprint planning and retrospective events became much more structured, and everybody grew confident with the process, the initial sprints were characterized by frustration, skepticism, and a feeling of chaos. It was clear that implementing Agile requires human-focused change management along the way, especially in the early days.

After a few sprints, we started seeing benefits, the best of which were around overall transparency, the sharing of work, and quicker removal of impediments. The lab technicians in particular placed great value on getting a better overview of the full picture and greater transparency into everybody's work. A key shift occurred in the move from pushing to pulling tasks: instead of the chemists directing lab technicians to do specific tasks, team members started taking responsibility for choosing their next tasks. The concept of MVP turned out to be a powerful way to foster good discussions, resolve impediments, and create learnings. The teams' mind-set was shifting!

After about six sprints, the benefits of Agile became very clear and the company decided to implement it in other molecular formulation teams within the development program. They have started discussing a product roadmap to outline MVPs for the next three to six months. As well, the teams are looking into conducting system demos for other departments every other month; doing that can capture early market and commercial feedback while developing new products, a process that traditionally takes six to twelve months.

Field Service Operations Center at a Commercial and Residential Energy Utility
(Contributed by Anthony Register, Business Agility Coach)

The operations center is responsible for field service work: taking work orders, dispatching technicians, managing equipment, and so on. For a long time, technicians experienced problems and inefficiencies in the course of their work, and customer feedback indicated dissatisfaction with service. The culture wasn't open to new ideas ("this is the way we always do things"), and as a result, morale and motivation were low. Leadership decided to have a special team focus on operational process improvement, with the goals of increasing employee engagement, improving customer satisfaction, and reducing costs. After seeing the technology organization's Agile transformation and the impact it had on the technologists, their business partners, and their customers, they decided to try approaching process improvement in an Agile way.

Leadership painted a picture of the vision: "As a field technician, when I arrive at work, my truck has everything I need to service my customers safely and then return to base." They prepared the stage for a learning environment, and committed to actively support the experiment for three months, in partnership with the Agile implementation team (of which I was a member). We hand-picked from the operations center 20 to 25 open-minded, motivated individuals who would remain dedicated full-time to the experiment. These were all people who were, or had been, directly involved with operations, such as procurement and vendor management specialists, schedulers, and front-line supervisors. Now, they were to be Agile team members focused on addressing the processes that they had previously lived with. We educated everyone on the "why" and "what" of Agile, choosing Scrum for the "how."

The team conducted focus groups with paying customers and field service workers, covering a variety of topics such as permits, materials, and scheduling. With everyone in a large open room (and using many sticky notes!) we mind-mapped all the input, organizing it into themes and groupings. Folks then self-selected into four Scrum teams of four to six people each. They wrote down work items related to process improvement, built backlogs, and made team agreements.

The four teams operated as Scrum teams for the next three months. They continuously interacted with the recipients of their process change ideas. Their sprint cycle was one week long; each sprint concluding with a review with leadership and a discussion of outcomes achieved and money saved. While they didn't conduct formal retrospectives, continuous improvement of their own work occurred on the fly as a result of conversations always going on. All teams worked in the same large room, which resulted in continuous open communication and flow of information between and across teams. I could see and feel the human energy! Very soon, the teams recognized the dependencies between them, and resolved them with a "Scrum of Scrums" meeting; they did so without suggestions or training from the coaches. As well, four sprints in, the teams decided to reorganize in order to rebalance the skills across the teams.

The team noticed a situation: the leadership group frequently brought them unplanned, high-priority requests that compromised their sprint plans. We couldn't influence this behavior, but had enough autonomy and safety to come up with a solution that leadership endorsed: when a request came in, a temporary team would form with individuals from each of the Scrum teams, would work together ("swarm") on the request from start to finish, and then the individuals would return to their original team.

After the first three months, the team's process waste reduction and removal effort yielded substantial bottom-line improvements (even after deducting the cost of the Scrum teams' work). Field workers had what they needed at the job site — equipment, material, permits, etc. — resulting in improved engagement, motivation, and morale. Customers indicated greater satisfaction with service delivery. The company used our approach as a guideline for other field service center locations. Leadership liked the results and extended the experiment by another three months. On a personal level, I feel fortunate to have been a contributor in this situation, where unusually high levels of autonomy, engagement, and participation with purpose resulted in palpable human energy and positive buzz.

ACKNOWLEDGMENTS

As with my previous works, I couldn't have written this book on my own. Many good souls helped make this book what it is by contributing to my research, by giving me feedback on early and advanced drafts, and by connecting me to others who did the same. These folks are: Omar Acuna, Chris Armstrong, Martin Aziz, Mike Bowler, Rob Brown, Liz Caspersen, Andy Cleff, Russ Dickerson, Thomas Friend, Ellen Grove, Yves Hanoulle, Arjay Hinek, Roger Hutcheson, Rebecca Jensen, Travis Klinker, Wolfgang Kohmann, Bernie Maloney, Jeanne Moster, Jeremy Pasley, Damon Poole, Jon Prosser, Jeremy Raleigh, Breanna Ramos, Anthony Register, David Spann, Joel Stone, Chris Taylor, Michael Thomassen, Darryl Vaz, Kendra West, and JoAnn White.

I'm especially grateful to six people who went the extra mile with their support: Andy Plattner, Kerstin Bresler, Claire Brown, Suzanne Daigle, Nick Heling, and John Hill.

As well, this book wouldn't exist without my non-software clients from the last few years. I'm thankful that they sought my guidance for becoming more Agile, and in the process helped expand my perspective on the world of work and the ways Agile can apply to diverse contexts.

I'm grateful to my wonderful family for their patience and support during the yearlong journey of writing this book. Credit for the cover artwork goes to my daughter, Galia, and as with all my professional work, my wife, Ronit, has been the best reviewer and collaborator.

Gil Broza
Toronto, 2019

NOTES

Chapter 1

1: *The Agile Manifesto* – http://agilemanifesto.org.

Chapter 2

1: Richard Sheridan, *Joy, Inc.: How We Built a Workplace People Love* (Portfolio, 2015).

2: Richard Sheridan, *Chief Joy Officer: How Great Leaders Elevate Human Energy and Eliminate Fear* (Portfolio, 2018).

3: This belief is congruent with the "Theory Y" of worker motivation, which along with "Theory X" was described in the 1960s. See this Wikipedia entry – https://en.wikipedia.org/wiki/Theory_X_and_Theory_Y.

4: The Cynefin Framework – https://en.wikipedia.org/wiki/Cynefin_framework – offers a typology of contexts that guides what sort of explanations or solutions might apply to a problem, situation, or system. It describes five domains, "complex" being one of them. The other four are obvious, complicated, chaotic, and disorder.

Chapter 3

1: *Beyond Budgeting* – https://bbrt.org.

Chapter 4

1: The output of this activity has many names, including charter, brief, and one-pager.

Chapter 5

1: Amy Edmondson, *The Fearless Organization: Creating Psychological Safety in the Workplace for Learning, Innovation, and Growth* (Wiley, 2018).

2: Shu-Ha-Ri is a sequential learning model that originated in martial arts. In Shu, the learner follows the teacher's instructions and focuses on proper execution. In Ha, the learner studies the theory and integrates it into his or her practice. In Ri, the learner is now a natural and makes his or her own rules.

Chapter 7

1: Chip Heath and Dan Heath, *The Power of Moments: Why Certain Experiences Have Extraordinary Impact* (Simon & Schuster, 2017).

2: Richard Sheridan, *Chief Joy Officer: How Great Leaders Elevate Human Energy and Eliminate Fear* (Portfolio, 2018).

3: Outcome thinking is not an Agile invention. It has gained popularity and inspired many techniques in the product and design fields. One example, similar to my description here, is the "Jobs to Be Done" theory; see Clayton Christensen and Michael Raynor, *The Innovator's Solution: Creating and Sustaining Successful Growth* (Harvard Business Review Press, 2003).

4: Henrik Kniberg offered this evolutionary progression as a replacement for the Minimal Viable Product (MVP) concept in a 2016 blog post. I have since taught it to many diverse clients, and found that it resonates well and helps build good habits.

5: Here is how this book evolved through Earliest Testable/Usable/Lovable:

Testable included three outcomes, which I worked on sequentially. The first was to figure out the book's topic and understand why I'd want to write it, both for readers and for myself. Then I needed to validate key hypotheses about the readers, such as how they might come to read the book. The third outcome was to determine the book's chapter structure and flow, because changing it mid-writing would be costly.

The Earliest Usable book had just enough to help the target reader get started with solid advice. It included 90% of the eventual text of chapters 1 through 10 and factored in feedback from five early readers. It had only some of the stories and no visuals, and did not undergo professional editing.

The Earliest Lovable book incorporated more feedback, examples, and stories; it included all the visuals, though they weren't polished; it had the appendices and the introduction.

I added a fourth evolutionary step, which I called the Earliest Polished book: that version included the foreword, cover art, testimonials, and print-grade visuals, and had undergone professional editing.

Contrast this evolution with output-based progress: "write business case. Prepare outline. Conduct field research. Write book. Design interior and cover. Copy editing."

6:   Technological development may affect ways of working more when it reduces the cost of change than when it reduces the cost of work. For example, think how easy it is for you to write large documents and emails, not because of replacing a pen with a keyboard, but because of easy cutting, copying, and pasting.

7:   Dr. Glenn Wilson, a University of London psychologist, led a study of "infomania" at Kings Psychiatry College — http://www. drglennwilson.com/Infomania_experiment_for_HP.doc. Employees jumping between several projects and experiencing constant distractions saw a 10-point fall in their IQ, the same effect as losing a night's sleep. For comparison, a group that smoked marijuana experienced half this IQ point drop.

Chapter 8

1:   This is known as "Gall's Law." Originally published in John Gall, *Systemantics: The Underground Text of Systems Lore* (General Systemantics Press, 1986).

2:   For general meeting facilitation, see Michael Wilkinson, *The Secrets of Facilitation: The SMART Guide to Getting Results with Groups* (Jossey-Bass, 2012). For Agile meeting facilitation, see Jean Tabaka, *Collaboration Explained: Facilitation Skills for Software Project Leaders* (Addison-Wesley Professional, 2006).

Chapter 9

1:   In this context, several Agile coaches like to use the now-paraphrased quote from the 19th century Prussian fieldmarshal Helmuth von Moltke the Elder: "No plan survives contact with the enemy."

2:   The latest edition of "A Guide to the Project Management Body of Knowledge" by the Project Management Institute has 756 pages — https://www.pmi.org/pmbok-guide-standards/foundational/pmbok.

3:   A popular technique is to note, on each small work item, when the team put it in the "Ready" column and when they finished working on it. Calculate the time difference between those points, and you have data for detecting trends, variance, and effects of attempted changes. For more, see chapter 11 in Marcus Hammarberg and Joakim Sunden, *Kanban in Action* (Manning, 2014).

4:   These ideas all come from the Kanban method. You can read about them in any current Kanban book. While they apply across all knowledge work, I haven't been able to locate a reference that explains the ideas using non-software development concepts and lingo.

5:   Are you wondering why I'm addressing this matter now, instead of when you designed the initial workflow? Because I wanted you to first have a solid mechanism for regular operations, which is hard enough to get right, rather than expect and legitimize interruptions from day one.

6: As explained in chapter 7, sprints (time-boxes) are another artificial way to constrain work intake that ought to stabilize the system and enable a sustainable pace. The popular term "velocity" indicates how much work the team does in an average sprint, and calculating it can help them plan to capacity. With its implications of speed, however, I've seen this term create bad dynamics and wrong interpretations of team Agility. If you use sprints, I suggest replacing "velocity" with the more neutral term "capacity."

7: Esther Derby and Diana Larsen, *Agile Retrospectives: Making Good Teams Great* (The Pragmatic Bookshelf, 2006); Patrick Kua, *The Retrospective Handbook: A Guide for Agile Teams* (Leanpub, 2012).

8: R. Brian Stanfield, *The Art of Focused Conversation: 100 Ways to Access Group Wisdom in the Workplace* (New Society Publishers, 2009).

9: The following questions trace the ORID sequence to elicit thoughtful feedback on emerging deliverables. You may want to adapt them to your situation, and probably use only some of them:

O: What did you observe? What did it do?

R: What did you like about it? What surprised you? What differed from your expectations? What would you have liked to see?

I: How would you use it? What other uses could it have? As we continue working on this, what should we watch out for? How does this simplify your work? What questions is this bringing up for you?

D: What should we change? What should we enhance? Which change is the highest priority? What should we not work on anymore?

10: John P. Kotter, *Leading Change* (Harvard Business Review Press, 2012); Esther Derby, 7 *Rules for Positive, Productive Change: Micro Shifts, Macro Results* (Berrett-Koehler Publishers, 2019).

Chapter 10

1: Fred Brooks made this observation in his 1986 paper, "No Silver Bullet." It is now reprinted in Fred Brooks, *The Mythical Man-Month: Essays on Software Engineering, Anniversary Edition* (Addison-Wesley Professional, 2018).

2: There are many good books on Lean thinking that focus on either manufacturing or development. For books on eliminating waste in business, see James P. Womack and Daniel T. Jones, *Lean Thinking: Banish Waste and Create Wealth in Your Corporation* (Free Press, 2003), and Linda M. Orr, *Eliminating Waste in Business: Run Lean, Boost Profitability* (Apress, 2014).

3: Tom DeMarco, *Slack: Getting Past Burnout, Busywork, and the Myth of Total Efficiency* (Broadway, 2002).

4: Patrick Lencioni, *The Ideal Team Player: How to Recognize and Cultivate the Three Essential Virtues* (Jossey-Bass, 2016). The three virtues are "humble," "hungry," and "smart."

5: Gil Broza, *The Human Side of Agile: How to Help Your Team Deliver* (3P Vantage Media, 2012); Heidi Helfand, *Dynamic Reteaming: How We Thrive by Rebuilding Teams* (Reteam, 2019).

6: For deep research, experience, and insights into metrics and measurements, read the blog of Troy Magennis — http://focusedobjective.com.

7: David J. Anderson and Alexei Zheglov, *Fit for Purpose: How Modern Businesses Find, Satisfy & Keep Customers* (Blue Hole Press, 2018).

8: In an example that made the news a few years ago, the Canada Revenue Agency (CRA) set itself a measurable goal: callers to its customer service center would be answered within two minutes. Here is a snippet from the independent auditor's report (http://www.oag-bvg.gc.ca/internet/English/parl_oag_201711_02_e_42667.html) of what happened as a result: "The Agency had a traffic team in each of its nine call centres. The teams were tasked with ensuring that wait times to speak with an agent did not exceed two minutes.

One of the ways the traffic team accomplished this was by blocking calls or directing them to the automated self-service system when the wait time approached two minutes. Blocked calls were any calls that did not reach either an agent or the automated self-service system. Callers who did not succeed in reaching an agent needed to redial the Agency if they still wished to speak with one."

9: A tool that several of my clients have found helpful is Gallup's Q12 Survey – https://q12.gallup.com.

10: See the "Health Checks for Teams and Leadership" blog post from Jimmy Janlen at Crisp – https://blog.crisp.se/2019/03/11/jimmy janlen/health-checks-for-teams-and-leadership; see also Sandy Mamoli and David Mole, *Creating Great Teams: How Self-Selection Lets People Excel* (The Pragmatic Bookshelf, 2015).

11: Shelle Rose Charvet, *Words That Change Minds: The 14 Patterns for Mastering the Language of Influence* (Institute for Influence, 2019).

12: Daniel Pink, in *Drive: The Surprising Truth About What Motivates Us* (Riverhead Trade, 2011), discusses autonomy, mastery, and purpose. In my unresearched opinion, enjoyability and challenge are also necessary conditions for motivation.

Epilogue

1: Jorgen Hesselberg, *Unlocking Agility: An Insider's Guide to Agile Enterprise Transformation* (Addison-Wesley Professional, 2018).

2: Agile Business Consortium – https://www.agilebusiness.org/page/WhatisBusinessAgility, accessed August 18, 2019.

Appendix: Stories from the Field

1: Jeff Patton, *User Story Mapping: Discover the Whole Story, Build the Right Product* (O'Reilly Media, 2014).

INDEX

An *n* following a page reference indicates information found in the notes.

from the Agile experiment, 33, 38, 159

M

managers
as decision-makers, 101, 113
as leaders, 67, 150–153, 171, 173
influencing people's behaviors, 18, 144–146, 171, 175
putting people first, 17, 68, 131, 140, 144
management
traditional approaches to, 27, 58–59, 91, 150, 169
matrix structure, 168
meetings. See touchpoints
meetings, facilitation, 131, 146
metrics, 169–171
minimum viable product (MVP), 194n7.
See also testable-usable-lovable
mind-set
defined, 9
significance of, 24, 26, 49–50, 56–59, 108
misalignment, 57–59
motivation
for Agile, 6, 62, 64, 136
of people, 77, 101, 122, 127, 175–176

N

O

obstacles. See impediments
ORID. See Focused Conversation Method
operational work, 14, 27, 39, 41, 96, 120
operating principles. See principles

optimizing [a way of working] for [certain values]. See value (meaning "important thing")
organizational agility. See business agility
outcomes (of work), 21, 41–42, 77, 79–82, 86, 98–99, 101, 112–113, 152

P

participation, 52, 109
performance
review/management, 28, 137, 175
of team, 75, 131, 168, 170
people before process. See managers putting people first
physical environment. See workspace
planning, 21, 55–56, 87–88, 90–92, 94–95, 124–125, 144–145
PO. See product owner
pod (synonym for a team), 108
policies
organizational, 101, 141
workflow, 130, 163
practices, 5, 8, 13, 27, 31, 56–57, 108–109, 172–173
predictability, 13, 19, 83, 101, 111
principles, 10–11, 22–23, 57–58, 71–72, 109, 110–111, 126, 152, 154–155, 167
prioritizing
values, 45
work, 87, 95, 113
process. See workflow
product, 12, 15, 36–37, 73, 75, 76–78, 129, 180
product backlog. See backlog
product owner (PO), 79, 113, 130, 131
productivity, 21, 94, 104–105, 120, 160

MEET GIL BROZA

Principal Agile Mentor and Owner, 3P Vantage, Inc.
Email contact: gbroza@3PVantage.com

Over the last 15 years, Gil has supported almost 100 large and small, private- and public-sector organizations along their Agile journeys. Seeking transformations, makeovers, or improvements, these clients have relied on his pragmatic, modern, and respectful guidance for customizing Agile in their contexts. Previously, Gil worked as a development manager, team leader, and programmer for many years, successfully applying Agile methods since 2001. He has served as a regular writer for the prestigious magazine *projectmanagement.com* (a PMI publication) and as a track chair for the Agile 2009, 2010, and 2016 conferences. He regularly gives keynotes and interactive talks at various conferences worldwide.

Throughout his career, Gil has focused on human characteristics that prevent positive outcomes in teams. These include limiting habits, fear of change, outdated beliefs, and blind spots, among many others. In helping teams overcome these factors, he supports them in reaching ever-higher levels of performance, confidence, and accomplishment. In

2012, he published *The Human Side of Agile*, the definitive guide to leading Agile teams. In 2015, he published *The Agile Mind-Set*, helping practitioners and leaders alike master the Agile approach and make their ways of working truly effective. With this book, Gil helps extend Agile transformations to nontechnical teams.

Gil provides training, coaching, consulting, facilitation services, and enablement programs to establish Agile ways of working, fix lackluster Agile attempts, and support ongoing Agile improvement efforts. In addition, he offers much-needed services to help managers, Scrum Masters, and team leaders grow as servant leaders. He is in high demand by organizations looking to fully realize Agile's potential. See his current offerings at 3PVantage.com/services.

www.ingramcontent.com/pod-product-compliance
Lightning Source LLC
Chambersburg PA
CBHW071422050326
40689CB00010B/1943